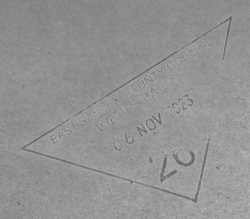

The Flavours of Andalucía

the Flavours of Andalucía

ELISABETH LUARD

GRUB STREET · LONDON

Published in 2017 by
Grub Street
4 Rainham Close
London
SW11 6SS

Email: food@grubstreet.co.uk
Web: www.grubstreet.co.uk
Twitter: @grub_street
Facebook: Grub Street Publishing

Printed and bound by Finidr, Czech Republic

Text and illustrations © Elisabeth Luard 1991, 2017
Copyright this edition © Grub Street 2017
First published by Collins & Brown Ltd, 1991
Cover and book design by Daniele Roa

A CIP catalogue record for this book is available
from the British Library.

ISBN 978-1-910690-48-2

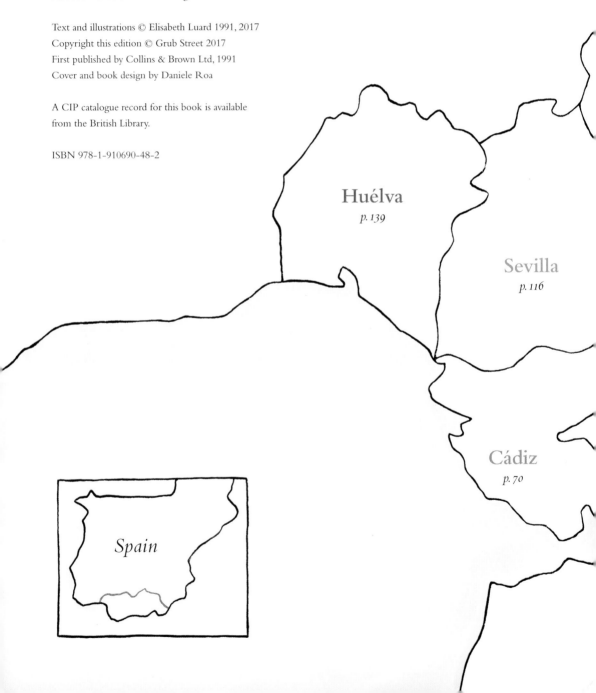

Huélva
p. 139

Sevilla
p. 116

Cádiz
p. 70

Spain

Contents

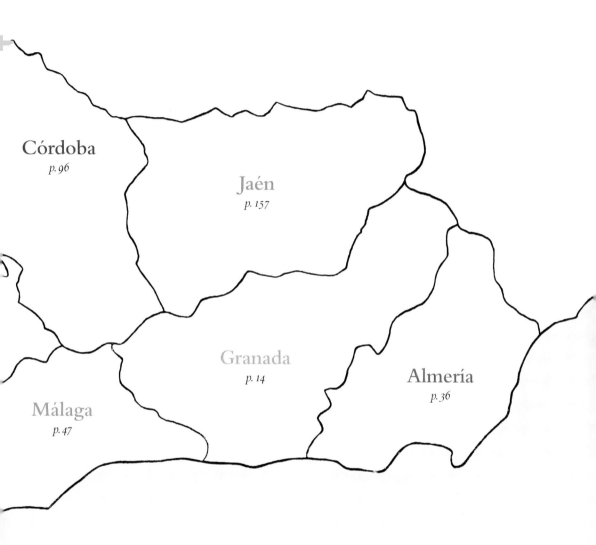

Mediterranean Sea

Introduction

THE ANDALUZ ARE BLESSED with *alegría*, that measure of contentment reached by having enough sunshine, a bit of good bread to fill the belly, an olive or two for the pleasure of it, a glass of wine to soothe the spirit, and a chair in the shade from which to watch the world go by. It all adds up to happiness. Happily, Andalucía was my home, and that of my growing family of four children, for twelve years.

The landscape holds the key. Here are golden hills lapped by silver seas, pearl-white valleys combed through with emerald vines, ochre-veined cliffs studded with pale-trunked cork-oaks and ebony-dark olive trees. And Andalucía, Spain's southernmost territory and the last area to be added to the kingdom of the Catholic Kings, Ferdinand and Isabel, is romantic – with its gypsy frills and haunting oriental music, its curved white arches and rainbow tiles, painted and brocaded wooden Virgins and black-hooded penitents.

It is always easier to be content when the sun shines and the land is fertile, but life in Andalucía has not come easy. Poverty there was – and, in lesser measure, still is. Greedy landowners and the ravages of war have seen to that. But with a patch of vines and a herb-scented hillside to scour for wild asparagus, a clutch of chickens to scratch in the yard, and maybe a chance, in the warm shallows of the shore, at landing a scoop of shrimps or a haul of sardines, the warm evenings are still a time for savouring the good things of life. There's time for the old men to set up a game of draughts in a corner of the café, and, in anticipation of supper, to fill the nostrils with the rich scent of garlic-laced stews which floats out of jasmine-fringed archways.

There's even a chance of an assignation, as the young people take their evening stroll around the square. Time for old grannies to sit, fingers flicking the crochet hook, and savour the time when they themselves were the stars of the twilight *paseo*. Time for the young matrons, one eye on their be-ribboned, lace-trimmed babies asleep in their prams, to settle down at a pavement table for a gossip, a glass of straw-pale wine and a slice of salty ham; or, perhaps, for a cup of hot chocolate and a sticky almond-flecked meringue, with a cone of sunflower seeds for the children to nibble.

Children, particularly small children, open all doors in Latin countries, and my four soon attracted attention. Our neighbours took pity on our urban ignorance and from them we quickly learned how to harvest our own tomatoes and peppers, how to spread the household linen on the grass so the sun and the chlorophyll could combine to bleach it clean as it dried. We were also told where to buy the best bread, who kept bees and would sell us honey, where and when to gather wild mushrooms and edible leaves, and how to collect the tiny summer snails which are so delicious simmered with Moorish spices. And instead of telling us what day the rubbish was collected, a small red piglet was installed in the rehabilitated pigsty at the end of the garden to recycle the household's vegetable peelings and leftovers. Some nine months later, the same neighbours turned up to guide me through the emotional process of turning piggy into hams and sausages.

Meanwhile, there was the market to tackle. To my urban eyes, the rings of stalls under Algeciras' domed marketplace were not a bit like the big-city supermarkets to which I was more accustomed. Poultry was only available on the hoof – forty years ago in this corner of Spain, no house-wife worth her sea salt would have trusted a dead chicken as far as she could chase it.

Nor was a young bird necessarily preferred: an old hen, past her laying-time, was reckoned the best meat for the slow-simmered one-pot stews which remain the mainstay of the Andaluz table. And I was taught that young birds, lacking in flavour what they gained in tenderness, were to be well garlicked and cooked with plenty of olive oil and sherry. I've never looked back – it's amazing what a heavy hand with the garlic can do for a bland supermarket bird.

The meat stalls were the most alarming of all. Lumps of unidenti-fiable meat either sliced into thin escalopes for frying, or sold in muscle-dictated hunks for adding to stews. Large slabs of grey unprocessed tripe and snakes of slithery black pudding were piled on white marble counters. Buckets of orange-coloured lard seemed to be sold by the scoop. Strung along a pole at head-height were those assorted bits and pieces that turn committed carnivores into vegetarians: liver and lights, kidneys and lungs, long pale torsos of milk-fed kid and furry rabbit and testicles, of course; the butcher took much pleasure in explaining their function and location to curious lady tourists.

Andalucía bien bebida y mal comida – Andalucía well-wined and ill-dined' – I had been told in Madrid and Barcelona and Valencia. But I did as my neighbours did, took advice and learned my lessons – and you eat very well in Andalucía, just so long as you go with the tide. The fish stalls were the most exciting: you never knew what you would find. Today's star attraction might be a giant swordfish or a fine pink-fleshed tuna, sliced into thin fillets to be slapped on the grill (broiler), and reckoned as good as steak. Tomorrow there might be a haul of emerald-flanked ruby-scaled mullet, glittering sardines and a fine trawl of prawns and shrimp – every purchaser would shove in an enquiring finger and lick it to see if over-brining betrayed too long a wait from ocean to slab. The children found the spectacle fascinating, a kind of endless street-theatre. In one corner there was usually a bucketful of sea urchins with an attendant small boy, no older than the eldest of my children, whose task it was to scoop the top off the prickly creature, and offer its orange interior as a restorative for exhausted shoppers.

The fruit and vegetable stalls were easier to decipher: piled high with whatever was in season – no flown-in lychees or out-of-season mangetouts here. From the first strawberries of spring to the last juicy oranges of the winter months, we never lacked for dessert. Not everything was familiar: there were creamy-fleshed custard apples with ebony pips, shiny-stoned loquats and persimmons, tart-pipped pomegranates, sticky green figs with scarlet flesh, passion fruit to be sucked from the skin, furry-skinned quince to be made into a thick opaque jelly for Christmas. And my neighbours showed me how to choose the special little round marrows for stuffing; which thin-fleshed peppers were perfect for frying; how to pick out the best tomatoes and the sweetest garlic; how to fritter the firm-fleshed aubergines and deep-fry the tiny artichokes, stalks and all; how to stew young broad beans in their pods.

Our house was buried in a cork-oak forest high above the straits of Gibraltar in the hills above the old Phoenician trading port of Tarifa. When the sea-mist lifted, we could see the mountains of Africa. It was across this narrow channel, guarded by the Pillars of Hercules, that the Moors sailed to conquer what seemed to them a rough, uncultured

bunch of infidels. They described the land they found as the antechamber to paradise. For seven centuries Andalucía was the jewel in the Muslim crown. Art and mathematics, literature and philosophy – both home-grown and imported – flourished under the patronage of the caliphs.

The Moors, too, perfected the irrigation systems first installed by the Romans, which still water Andalucía's market gardens. The easterners' long reign is commemorated in the architecture and names of Andalucía's whitewashed villages: Benarraba, Medina Sidonia, Alhaurín, Benalaura, Algatocín. Gibraltar itself is the Moorish 'Jebl Tariq'. The shifting frontiers between Muslim and Christian powers can be clearly plotted in the string of citadels which hold the mountain passes: Jimena de la Frontera, Arcos, Morón, Castellar. You can see the oriental hand, too, in the spices with which all Andaluz cooks instinctively and confidently season their dishes: saffron and cloves, nutmeg and cinnamon, cumin and peppercorns. Above all, Moorish tastes are kept alive in the Andaluz love of sweet things: a thousand and one rich little confections of egg yolk and sugar, meringue and candied fruit; the honey and almond *halvas* and sweet nut milks; and those sticky, feathery pastries which are the national passion – made daily and sold warm and caramel-scented to eager queues in every little village confectioner's.

If the Moors' influence is most easily traced in the knowledge and skills they encouraged and imparted, it was the New World which filled Andalucía's store cupboard. Tomatoes, peppers, beans, pumpkins, marrows, maize, chocolate and vanilla were unknown in the Old World before 1492. All were first unloaded on to Andalucía's busy quaysides from the galleons that followed the charts redrawn by Christopher Columbus. The mighty potato, destined to fuel Europe's population explosions of the eighteenth and nineteenth centuries, was first admired for its pretty papery flowers on the patios of Sevilla's aristocratic ladies. The fertile soil of Andalucía made a fine nursery for the new arrivals – and the cooks of Andalucía were not slow to use their skills in preparing them.

Underlying these acquired tastes is a more ancient tradition: the cookery of the peasantry – slow to change, dependent on landscape and availability of fuel, limited by seasonality and proximity to trade routes. Rural housewives have easy access to the finest local or home-produced raw materials, and spend their hard-earned cash with care. Certain places became locally celebrated for particular produce – the wind-dried hams of Jabugo and Trevelez, the sheep's cheese of Grazalema, the tiny flatfish *(acedias)* caught round the mouth of the Guadalquivir; perfect peaches from this particular village, the finest plums and the best almonds from that hillside.

Bread and pulses make up the bulk of the countryman's diet. Fresh vegetables are usually included as an integral part of a dish, although sometimes they are presented on their own, as an accompaniment – fried, frittered or stewed in olive oil, as a kind of ratatouille. Peas, beans and wild asparagus are often cooked with eggs to make a tortilla, a thick, solid omelette. Greens such as spinach, chard and a wide range of wild leaves go into the pot to add freshness to a bean stew.

Salads are usually simple and plainly dressed: ripe tomatoes cut into chunks and sprinkled with chopped garlic and olive oil; cos lettuce and the mildest onion sliced and tossed in salt, oil and lemon juice.

Down by the coast, the wives of fishermen are adept at turning that part of the catch which cannot easily be exchanged for ready money (the cheaper, more perishable fish – sardines, anchovies, small flatfish) into nourishing fish soups. In rice-growing areas – and most of Andalucía's provinces have pockets of these – a bit of wild game or chicken and a pinch of saffron is likely to be turned

into a rice-with-broth dish for the whole family, with paella, prepared al fresco by the father of the family, as the favourite Sunday lunch. Gazpachos – bread porridges – are the upland equivalent of the rice dishes of the littoral. Some farms still make their own cheese and keep a pig or two to stock their winter storecupboard; and many Andaluz housewives brine and flavour their own olives.

Cheese, home-pickled olives, chorizo (*pimentón*-spiced sausage) and ham are the tapas – the little titbits or obligatory 'lids' for a glass of cold dry sherry or wine – you are most likely to hand round at home. In a bar, particularly one with a restaurant attached, the tapas will be more ambitious, and each establishment is known for its own specialities. Nowadays in the big cities and resorts you have to pay for a plateful (a *ración*) to share among friends. But sometimes, with luck, and when you're off the tourist track, the titbit comes included in the price of a glass of wine – and you take what you are given. Whatever the deal, tapa bars offer a cheap and convivial way of sampling a range of local recipes. You often get a dab of the restaurant's dish of the day, and maybe a grilled sardine or marinated anchovy if the fishermen have had a fair wind. Tapa bars in big cities, such as Sevilla,

serve luxurious seafood – prawns, crabs, clams, lobsters – which they sell by weight, and prepare to order for their customers. Such places are always crowded at festival time. Small villages offer more simple pleasures: a slice of chorizo or morcilla sausage, a square of potato tortilla, even a delicate little croquette or a tiny kebab.

The Spaniard likes his food identifiable and uncluttered, with griddle and frying-pan the chief culinary apparatus. Meat is prefered sauced with its own juices, fish and shellfish are prized for their taste of the sea. In Andalucía, the best of home-grown raw materials are prepared with one or all of the three most important native ingredients: olive oil, wine and garlic. The most widely used herbs are the great aromatics of the Mediterranean – thyme, rosemary, fennel, oregano and bay – with plenty of parsley of the flat-leaved 'Italian' variety and, in Moorish strongholds, mint.

There are eight Andalucían provinces, each with its own distinctive character – its culinary identity dictated by geography and, above all, the extent to which the sybaritic

Moors took charge of the cooking pots. Delicious Granada, star in the crown of the Moorish caliphs and the last province to fall to the Catholic Kings, is famed for its fertile plateau, watered by the snow-fed streams of the mountains of the Sierra Nevada. Almería, with its pale sands, red cliffs and enclosed green valleys, was once a pirate stronghold and is the most easterly of Andalucía's provinces. Málaga, centred on the busy port of the same name, has a hinterland rich in vineyards, nut-groves and orchards, though it is probably best known to sun- and sea-lovers for its long Mediterranean beaches backed by high-rise developments. The silvery coast of Cádiz, its beaches pounded by the rolling breakers of the Atlantic, boasts trading ports made rich by trade with the New World. Córdoba is doubly blessed with its rich farmland and graceful flower-decked capital. Gilded Sevilla with its rich wheatfields, has a chief city that was the natural capital of Andalucía and treasure-house of the Americas. Tucked away in the western corner is mineral-rich Huelva, which counts among its blessings the dark mountains of the Sierra Morena, and much of the bird-rich wetland of the Guadaliquivir's wide delta. And finally there is upland Jaén, threshold to La Mancha, dominated by a rocky plateau starred with olive groves and some of the prettiest towns in the whole of Spain.

Andalucía's provinces all have their own recipes for *alegría*. Here are just a few of them. As the old Andaluz greeting has it: *buen proveche*, good appetite.

Elisabeth Luard

Granada

The spirit of the Moors lives on in the kitchens of Granada, and the cookery of the ancient kingdom of the caliphs remains among the best in Spain. This, the most romantic of Andalucía's cities, was the jewel in the Muslim crown; Christians, Jews and Muslims flourished in harmony under the enlightened rulers of the Nasrid dynasty, and all contributed their expertise to the culinary traditions of the city they called the Gateway to Paradise.

The sybaritic easterners brought snow from the Sierra Nevada to cool their sherbets; imported spices and grew saffron to spice their *al-cuscuzu;* irrigated the surrounding plain and planted almonds and aubergines, broad beans and artichokes, figs, oranges, lemons, grapes and rice.

Granada was the last Moorish stronghold to fall to the Catholic Kings as they reconquered Spain. The boy-sultan Boabdil fled the combined might of Ferdinand of Aragon and Isabel of Castile in the same year that Columbus sailed west in search of a new spice route to the East. He returned with a cargo of New World vegetables, and before long potatoes and peppers, tomatoes and maize, beans and marrows were planted in the market gardens, providing a seed-bed for the rest of Europe.

Today, the ethereal Alhambra, with its intricate arabesques, ice-white halls, marble-ducted snow-water streams, sky-bright pools and lush, shady gardens, soars above the solid granite-grey Spanish city which replaced the Arab souks and silk markets.

THE FLAVOURS OF ANDALUCÍA

Exotic as a belly dancer in a downtown rush hour, the caliphs' palace is a reminder of the artistic and architectural skill of the vanished conquerors.

Granadinos still have the eastern taste for mixing the sensual with the spiritual, and maintain literary-gastronomic societies not unlike the more down-to-earth men-only dining clubs of the Basques, to whose territories many of Granada's Moriscos, its converted Moors, were exiled in the 1500s.

As for home-cooking, the city remains true to her patrician origins and keeps a rich bourgeois table. The cheaper cuts of meat and offal furnish the urban poor and the gypsies of Sacromonte with more modest delicacies, and these too are given eastern spicing. The sweetmaking of the Arabs became the province of Christian nuns, who baked delicious confections for saints' days.

There is no wine to speak of: this is not vine-country, and followers of the Prophet were not permitted strong drink. Water is another matter: the springs of the Sierra Nevada supplied the citizens with the clearest, purest and most delicious of refreshment. The legacy of the Moors remains, too, in

Granada's magnificent fruit and vegetables. Even its *bouquet garni*, the *ramillete alabaicinero*, is a Moorish combination of mint, parsley and bay leaves. These days it flavours soups and stews enriched with Christian pork, prohibited by both Jewish and Muslim law: but providing proof, if any further was needed, that many cooks make fine broth.

Sopa de almendras
Almond soup

8oz/250g/1½ cups
  blanched almonds
6 tablespoons olive oil
2 slices stale bread, cubed
12 garlic cloves, skinned
  and roughly chopped
2-3 parsley sprigs,
  roughly chopped
1 teaspoon cumin seeds
6-8 saffron threads
1½ pints/900ml/3¾ cups
  water
Salt and pepper

To finish
Garlic croutons
A few slivered almonds,
  toasted

Serves 4

Sopa de almendras *is not like the Christmas soup of Castile
that goes by the same name, but a Moorish mixture of ground
almonds, pepper, cumin, saffron, garlic, parsley and fried bread.
Almonds planted by the Moors still add grace to the cookery of
Granada. The thickening of soups and sauces with bread is an
ancient technique – perhaps it comes naturally to those the
Romans nominated the best bakers in their empire.*

Warm the olive oil in a small frying-pan (skillet). When it is
hot, add the almonds, half the bread cubes, the garlic and
parsley, and let it all brown gently but thoroughly.

Either pound the mixture to a paste with the cumin and the
saffron in a pestle and mortar, or tip the contents of the
frying-pan, plus the cumin and saffron, into the food
processor and process it with a little water to a smooth paste.

Transfer the paste to a saucepan and stir in the water. Bring
gently to the boil, turn down the heat and simmer the soup
for 5 minutes. Take it off the heat and stir in the
remaining bread cubes. Add salt and pepper. Cover
and leave it for 10 minutes on the side of the stove
for the bread to become spongy.

Serve the soup with hot garlic croutons
and a few toasted slivered almonds.

Potaje de San Antón

Broad bean soup with tripe

**1lb/500g dried broad
beans, soaked for
at least 8 hours or
overnight**
8oz/250g prepared tripe
**1 pig's trotter (and an ear
and a tail if you can
get them)**
1–2 garlic cloves
6–8 saffron threads
**6oz/175g thickly cut
dry-cured streaky
bacon, cubed**
**1 onion, skinned and
chopped**
1 bay leaf
1 marjoram sprig
Salt and pepper

To finish
**4oz/125g morcilla or
other black pudding,
thinly sliced**
1 mint sprig, chopped
1 parsley sprig, chopped

Serves 4

*Until the arrival of the New World haricots, broad beans were the
winter stores of Europe – as they were of North Africa, where
there are a great many dishes made with fava beans, including
falafel. In this rich winter soup from the Alpujarras, the beans are
enriched with the cheaper cuts of the pig – prohibited meat under
the Moors, but in these Christian times the mainstay of the
cookery of Andalucía.*

Drain and rinse the soaked beans and put them in a large
saucepan with enough cold water to cover them to a depth
of two fingers.

Cut the tripe into squares. Rinse and scald the pig's trotter.

Hold the garlic cloves in a naked flame until they are lightly
charred. Roast the saffron for a few moments in a spoon held
over the flame.

Put all the ingredients, except the morcilla and chopped herbs,
in the pan with the beans. Add salt and pepper. Bring to the
boil, turn down the heat, cover and leave to simmer gently for
3-4 hours, either on the top of the stove or in a very low oven.
Add more boiling water if
necessary. Taste and adjust
the seasoning.

Slip the slices of morcilla
into the soup and
finish with a sprinkle
of the fresh green
herbs.

Habas a la granadina
Broad bean and artichoke hot-pot

**1lb/500g young broad
   beans in the pod
   (or 12oz/375g podded
   beans)**
**2 large artichokes
   (or 6 tiny violet ones)**
6 tablespoons olive oil
**2 garlic cloves, skinned
   and chopped**
**1 large onion, skinned
   and finely chopped**
**8oz/250g tomatoes,
   scalded, skinned and
   chopped**
**Small bunch of parsley,
   mint and bay leaf**
Salt and pepper
**1 tablespoon fresh
   breadcrumbs**
3-4 saffron threads
½ teaspoon cumin seeds
1 teaspoon *pimentón*

To finish (optional)
1-2 eggs per person

*Serves 4 as a starter, 2 as a
   vegetarian main course*

*This is Granada's favourite midday meal-in-a-pot made with the
fine vegetables from the rich* huertas *(market gardens) first
planted by the Moors. At the beginning of the season, broad
beans can be cooked whole with their pods – they have a delicious
smoky flavour somewhere between okra and asparagus. Moorish
spicing gives the dish its distinctively Granadine character.*

If the beans are young enough to use whole, string them and
chop them into short lengths as for runner beans. If they are
older, they will have to be podded.

If you are using large artichokes, cut off the stalks, peel off the
tough outer strings, and chop the stalks into short lengths.
Trim the outside leaves of the artichokes right down to the
base, leaving the tender inner leaves, and cut the artichokes
into quarters. Nick out the exposed feathery choke with a
sharp knife. Small artichokes need only to be washed and
trimmed – slightly larger ones should be halved and the
choke removed. If you prepare them ahead, rub the cut sides
with lemon to prevent them blackening.

Warm all but 2 tablespoons of the oil in a frying-pan
(skillet), add the finely chopped garlic and onion, and let
the vegetables sweat until they soften and take a
little colour. Add the skinned, chopped tomatoes,
turn up the heat, and let it all bubble up into
a rich thick sauce.

Meanwhile, put the prepared beans, artichokes and stalks into a large saucepan with enough cold salted water to cover them. Bring them quickly to a rolling boil, and then drain them immediately.

Tip the tomato sauce into the pan with the beans and artichokes, add enough water to submerge the vegetables, tuck in the herbs and season with salt and pepper. Bring to the boil, cover the pan and put it to simmer over a low heat for 30-40 minutes, until about half the juices have been absorbed and the vegetables are nearly tender. This can be done in the oven if you prefer, at 300°F, 180°C, Gas Mark 4 for 50-60 minutes.

Meanwhile, heat the remaining oil in the frying-pan, and stir in the breadcrumbs. When they are golden, sprinkle in the saffron, cumin and *pimentón*. Remove the pan from the heat, and mash the contents together. Stir this aromatic mixture into the bean pot and let everything simmer for another 5-10 minutes.

If you would like a more substantial dish, make dents in the surface of the stew with the back of a ladle, and slide in an egg for each person. Replace the lid and simmer for 5 minutes more, to set the eggs lightly. Nervous souls can fry or poach the eggs separately.

Serve each helping topped with an egg, and provide plenty of good bread to mop up the juices.

Fritos de verduras
Green fritters

**1lb/500g fresh spinach
and spring greens
(or use frozen)**
4 tablespoons olive oil
**6-8 spring onions
(scallions), trimmed
and chopped**
**½ teaspoon grated
nutmeg**
Salt and pepper
3 eggs

To finish
1 egg, lightly beaten
**4-5 heaped tablespoons
breadcrumbs**
Oil for frying

Serves 4

*Vegetables are almost always served as a separate course in
Andalucía, either as a prelude to the main, meat dish or, particularly in rural areas where the ingredients are all home-grown, as
the main dish itself. The Andaluz rural housewife likes to use eggs
from her own hens, scraps of* jamón serrano *(cured ham) and rich
green olive oil to add flavour and substance to the products of her*
huerta, *the garden patch which all rural housewives cultivate.*

Rinse, pick over and shred the fresh leaves. Cook them in a
lidded pan with a little salt and the minimum of water for
about 5 minutes only. Frozen leaf spinach must be defrosted
first. Drain the greens well and shred them roughly.

Heat 2 tablespoons of the oil in an omelette pan and add the
chopped spring onions (scallions). Fry for a few minutes until
they soften and gild, and then stir in the shredded greens.
Season with nutmeg, salt and pepper. Turn the greens in the
heat, and steam off some of their moisture. Take them off the
heat and let them cool a little.

Mix the eggs lightly together with a fork, and then stir in the
cooled greens.

Heat the remaining oil in the pan and pour in the egg
mixture. Fry it gently as a thick pancake or tortilla (a firm, flat
omelette), turning once – easiest done with courage and a
plate for reversing it back into the pan. You may have to make
two – it all depends on the size of your pan. Let the tortilla or
tortillas cool, and then cut into squares.

Heat a deep frying-pan (skillet) of oil. Dip the tortilla
squares in the egg and then coat them with
breadcrumbs, and fry until golden. They're
lovely with a fresh tomato sauce.

Tortilla Sacromonte

Gipsy omelette

1 lamb's brain
2-3 lamb sweetbreads
  and/or *criadillas*
  (testicles), if available
½ small onion, skinned
1 parsley sprig
1 bay leaf
A few peppercorns
2 tablespoons milk
  beaten with a little egg
2 tablespoons
  breadcrumbs
3-4 tablespoons olive oil
1 large potato, peeled
  and cut into small
  cubes (omit if you have
  plenty of offal)
2 lamb's kidneys, skinned,
  cored and thinly sliced
2oz/50g *jamón serrano*
  cured ham, or pancetta,
  finely chopped
1 tablespoon chopped red
  pepper
1 tablespoon shelled peas
  (fresh or frozen)
4 eggs
Salt

Serves 4 as a starter

This celebrated tortilla is a speciality of the Sacromonte, the cave-dwelling gypsy quarter in the cliffs opposite the Alhambra. It features the variety of meats that have long been a cheap source of protein for the urban poor. On the day of the patron saint, the authorities make obeisance with flowers and incense, and are rewarded with slices of this tortilla.

Soak the brain and sweetbreads (and testicles, if you can get them) for a few hours. Put them in a saucepan with the onion, parsley, bay leaf and peppercorns, and enough lightly salted water to cover. Bring to the boil, then simmer gently for about 20 minutes, until they are firm and cooked through. Drain and leave to cool between two plates. Skin and slice the meats, removing any visible tubes. Egg-and-breadcrumb the slices and fry them in a little of the oil in a frying-pan (skillet) until lightly browned. Drain in a sieve.

Meanwhile, heat the rest of the oil in a small omelette pan. Add the potato cubes, if using. Cook until soft, but not browned. Drain in a sieve over a small basin and reheat the oil in the frying-pan. Fry the kidneys, ham or gammon, and chopped red pepper until lightly browned. Add the peas.

Beat the eggs lightly with a little salt. Add the meats, red pepper, peas and drained potatoes. Pour most of the oil out of the pan, leaving only a tablespoon or two. Return the pan to the heat and tip in the egg mixture. Fry gently on a low heat until the eggs begin to set. With a spatula, push everything down into the egg so that it is all submerged. As the tortilla cooks, build up a deep straight edge with the spatula. When firm, slide it on to a plate, invert it back into the pan and cook the other side. Don't overcook it – the centre should be juicy.

Serve warm or cool, cut into bite-sized cubes.

Remojon
Orange salad

This salad can be classed as a sort of gazpacho: eaten in winter and spring, when there is no fresh tomato or appetite for a gazpacho. It is traditionally made with salt cod, bacalao, the universal fasting food in mountain districts of Catholic countries. If you have bacalao, soak it for a few hours, grill it fiercely for a few minutes, then shred and bone it with the fingers. Salt cod is now so expensive that salted tuna and anchovies, sometimes with hard-boiled eggs, are commonly used as a replacement.

6 oranges
1 small can tuna
   (about 4oz/125g)
1 small can anchovies
4 tablespoons olive oil
1 red pepper, hulled,
   de-seeded and sliced
   lengthwise
6-8 spring onions
   (scallions)
1 garlic clove, skinned
   and crushed with a
   little salt
1 tablespoon wine or
   sherry vinegar
2oz/50g pickled green
   olives

Serves 4 as a starter

Peel the oranges with a sharp knife, taking care to remove all the pith, and cut them in fine slices. Drain and flake the tuna. Separate the anchovies, drain them and reserve the oil for the dressing.

Heat the olive oil gently in a frying-pan (skillet). Put in the red pepper strips and let them fry for about 10 minutes, until they soften and caramelize a little. Take care not to overheat the oil.

Put the orange slices in a bowl, and toss with the contents of the frying-pan, the chopped spring onions (scallions), the garlic crushed in a little salt, and vinegar. Finish with the flaked tuna, the anchovies and their oil, and the olives.

Leave the salad to marinate for 1-2 hours. Serve with crisp lettuce leaves to act as scoops.

Caracoles en salsa con almendras
Snails in tomato sauce with almonds

4 dozen ready-cooked snails (in their shells or out of them)

For the sauce
3-4 tablespoons olive oil
1 onion, skinned and finely sliced
2oz/50g/½ cup blanched almonds
2oz/50g/½ cup pine kernels
1 teaspoon *pimentón*
6-8 saffron threads, soaked in a splash of boiling water (or 1 teaspoon ground saffron)
1 fennel sprig, chopped
1 mint sprig, chopped
8oz/250g tomatoes, scalded, skinned and chopped (or use canned)
1 glass white wine
Salt and pepper

Serves 4 as a starter

Two kinds of snail are gathered in Andalucía – the large ones familiar from the French snail dishes, descendents of the Roman snail farms, and tiny winkle-sized creatures which do not hibernate, but aestivate on thorny thistles through the summer, taking advantage of the spines to give them protection against hungry goldfinches. Large snails will need about two weeks' starvation in a loosely-lidded bucket to cleanse their systems (the smaller ones need only a few days). They should then be washed thoroughly in several changes of clear cold water, alternating with a good salting to get rid of the goo. When they are well cleaned, bring them gently to the boil in clean water flavoured with peppercorns, a bay leaf, coriander seeds, garlic cloves, spearmint and a dried chilli. When the water froths up, throw in a spoonful of vinegar to cut the foam. Simmer the snails for 1-1½ hours.

Alternatively, substitute lamb's hearts, trimmed of fat and veins, sliced and simmered in stock until tender, then cut into snail-sized cubes – the texture and flavour is enough like the real thing to fool many a customer enjoying what he imagines to be escargots à la bourguignonne *in a French bistro.*

Heat the oil in a shallow pan and gently fry the onion until it softens and gilds.

Push the onion to one side and brown the almonds and pine kernels in the hot oil. Add the *pimentón*, saffron, herbs and tomatoes. Bubble up until the sauce thickens. Add the wine and salt and pepper and let it bubble up again.

Add the snails and bring back to the boil. Cover and cook gently for 30–40 minutes to develop all the flavours, then serve.

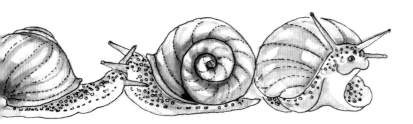

Potaje de lentejas a la granadina
Farmhouse lentil soup

1lb/500g green-brown lentils (not the yellow Indian ones)

1 fine quince or a piece of marrow, peeled and cut into chunks

2 tablespoons olive oil

2 garlic cloves, left in their skins and singed in a flame

A short length of *jamón serrano* ham bone or a small bacon hock

2 tablespoons chopped mint

2 tablespoons chopped parsley

1 teaspoon ground saffron

1 teaspoon *pimentón*

1-2 dried red chillies, or 1 teaspoon cayenne

1 bay leaf

2 firm pears, cored and cubed

2-3 spring onions (scallions), chopped

Salt

Serves 4-6

Lentils – the greeny-brown variety – are one of Andalucía's favourite storecupboard staples. They are the fast food of the pulse tribe. In this version of the classic soup-stew, the difference comes from the rather Moorish inclusion of fruit.

Pick over the lentils and remove any tiny stones. Put the lentils and all the other ingredients, except the pears, spring onions (scallions) and salt, in a large saucepan. Add enough water to submerge everything to a depth of two fingers.

Bring the pan to a rolling boil, turn down the heat, cover loosely and leave to simmer gently for 1 hour, adding boiling water if necessary, until the lentils are soft and the quince is perfectly tender. Taste and add salt.

Stir in the pears and the spring onions (scallions) – and reheat for a moment only, unless the pears are very hard and need a little stewing, before serving.

Espetón de sardinas
Spitted sardines

**2lb/1kg fresh medium-
sized sardines**
**A bundle of bamboo
canes (used as wind-
breaks in the irrigated
huertas, or vegetable
gardens)**
Sea salt

Serves 4

*The fishing port of Motril likes its sardines spitted whole and
grilled over hot coals on the beach. This is strictly a seaside feast,
and the fish must be of the freshest. Sardines need no basting as
they have plenty of their own fat just under the skin.*

*Motril deals in sugar cane – so you can suck a stick of it while
the cooking-fire burns up. If you want to adapt this recipe for
cooking at home, the sardines can be put on metal skewers and
cooked on a barbecue for the same length of time.*

Dig a narrow trench 3 feet/1 metre long in the sand, and light
a driftwood fire in it. When there are no longer any flames
and it has burned down to hot coals, it is ready for cooking.
Sharpen the bamboo canes at both ends.

Rinse the fish in sea water – most of the scales will come off
by rubbing, but it doesn't matter if some are left. Do not gut
them or remove the heads. Spike the sardines through the
middle, taking care the spike goes through the spine. Sprinkle
the fish with sea salt.

Stick the bamboo skewers upright in the sand, leaning them
over the trench of coals. The thicker the fish the longer they
will need – 3-4 minutes a side should be ample. Eat them
with your fingers straight off the canes.

Perdices en pobre

Poacher's partridges

Behind the date-palms and prickly pears of Granada's coastal strip rise the rocky slopes of the Alpujarras – wild rough mountainside with few villages and a primitive culture. Bandit-country in the old days, this was the last stronghold of the Granada caliphs. The heights are patrolled by eagles and vultures, and thick cistus and broom scrub shelters their prey – providing, too, one of the last haunts of the cabra hispanica, *Europe's native wild goat. This is a poacher's dish: the inhabitants of these remote crags were not particular about whose game they snared. Partridges were attracted by their caged fellows – traitor-birds set out in the scrub to call up their own kind.*

3 partridges, cleaned and halved
Salt and pepper
4 tablespoons olive oil
2 garlic cloves, skinned and chopped
1 lemon, diced
4 tablespoons chopped parsley

Serves 4-6

Wipe over the birds and season them with salt and pepper. Heat the oil in a flameproof earthenware casserole or heavy frying-pan (skillet). Put in the halved birds with their hearts and livers, and fry them gently, turning once, until they are golden-brown all over.

Sprinkle in the garlic, diced lemon and parsley, and let them take a little colour. Pour in enough water to nearly submerge the birds and bubble it all up. Turn down the heat and simmer gently, basting regularly, for 30 minutes or so, until the birds are tender and the juices have reduced down to an aromatic oil.

You will need no other embellishment but bread and a salad. To conclude the meal, the Alpujarras have grapes and fresh ripe figs.

Conejo al ajillo
Rabbit with garlic

1 rabbit, jointed and cut into bite-sized pieces
1 tablespoon seasoned flour
8 tablespoons olive oil
12 fat garlic cloves, unskinned but flattened a little with a knife
1-2 thyme sprigs
1 glass water or white wine

Serves 4

Another poacher's dish — and very good it is too. The plump little rabbits fatten up on the scented herbs and sage-brush, and provide many a poor farmer with food for free. You can tell if the rabbit is a young 'un if the ears tear easily. All hunters should be able to skin their own rabbits, just as all fishermen should be able to scale and gut their own fish.

Lightly dust the rabbit pieces with seasoned flour. Heat the olive oil in a heavy frying-pan (skillet). Put in the rabbit and turn the pieces in the hot oil until they are well browned. Add the garlic cloves after a few minutes and let them take a little colour. Add the thyme and pour in the water or wine. Let it all bubble up.

Turn down the heat, cover loosely and leave to simmer gently on a low heat for 30-40 minutes, depending on the age of the rabbit, until the meat is cooked through but still moist and tender, and the juices have practically evaporated, leaving a deliciously garlicky oil as the sauce.

Serve with thick-cut chips, Andaluz-style. And of course, no Spaniard would take a meal without bread.

Liebre con andrajos
Hare with noodle-dumplings

1 young hare, paunched
   and skinned
1 tablespoon olive oil
1 bay leaf
Salt and pepper
1 glass red wine
About 2 pints/1.2 litres/
   5 cups water

For the dumplings
12oz/350g/3 cups plain
   (all-purpose) flour
1 tablespoon salt
1 tablespoon olive oil
½ pint/200ml/⅔ cup
   water

For the sauce
4 tablespoons olive oil
1 onion, skinned and
   finely chopped
1 garlic clove, skinned
   and finely chopped
1lb/500g tomatoes,
   scalded and skinned
   (or use canned)
1 teaspoon *pimentón*

To finish
1 tablespoon
   dried crushed
   mint

Serves 4–8, depending
* on the size of the hare*

Andalucía has a great variety of savoury wheat-flour porridges – Andrajos, ajo harina, gachas – fortifying fuel-food which antedates the rice dishes of the Romans and Moors, and belongs instead to the most ancient traditions of European cookery. The genre includes not only flour-thickened soups, but also dumplings and noodles – it is all a matter of the taste and skill of the cook, in making milled grain palatable. You can use macaroni instead of the dumpling dough if you prefer. This recipe comes from the Alpujarras, where the wild game still has the run of the sage-brush.

Remove the fine membrane which covers the back and hind legs and joint the hare into 12-16 small pieces. Put them in a saucepan with the oil, bay leaf, salt and pepper, and wine, and enough water to cover. Bring the pan to the boil, then let it simmer gently for 50-60 minutes, until the meat is falling off the bone. Add more boiling water if necessary.

Meanwhile, make the dumplings. Sieve the flour into a large bowl with the salt. Work in the oil and enough water to make a soft dough. Work the dough well. On a board, roll it out very very thinly, then cut it into smallish squares.

Take the meat off the bone and reserve it. Save the meat stock – there should be about 1 pint/600 ml/2½ cups.

To make the sauce, warm the oil in the saucepan and add the onion and garlic. Fry for a few minutes. Add the tomatoes and *pimentón* and bubble it all up to thicken the sauce. Dilute it with the meat stock and add the hare pieces. Reheat, and slip in the dumplings – add extra boiling water to submerge them. Simmer for 5-6 minutes, until the dumplings are soft.

Finish with a sprinkling of mint. Serve in deep plates, with a fork and spoon and bread, accompanied by a chilled glass of the local wine, the dry rosé of Albondón.

Albóndigas de gallina y jamón

Chicken and ham meatballs

½ **boiling fowl (to yield about 8oz/250g meat)**
1 *jamón serrano* **ham bone or bacon knuckle**
Small bunch of parsley, mint and bay leaf
A few peppercorns
1 **teaspoon ground saffron**
Grated zest and juice of ½ lemon
6oz/175g **fatty** *jamón serrano* **cured ham or fat bacon**
3 **eggs, forked together**
4-5 **heaped tablespoons breadcrumbs, soaked and squeezed dry**
1-2 **tablespoons chopped parsley**
1 **garlic clove and ½ onion, skinned and finely chopped**
Salt and pepper
2-3 **tablespoons olive oil**

This recipe from Montefrio, high in the hills above Granada, has Greek undertones in its lemon and egg-yolk thickening. Meatballs are the shepherd's pie of the Andaluz kitchen: good cheap family food. Moulding neat little albóndigas *is the first task small children, eager to help mother, are allotted.*

Strip the meat from the bird and reserve it. Put the bones, including the ham or bacon bone, in a saucepan with about 2 pints/1.2 litres/5 cups water, with the herbs, peppercorns, saffron and lemon zest and juice. Bring it to the boil, then simmer for an hour or so, to make a strong stock.

Mince the chicken meat finely with the ham or bacon. Work the meat, eggs, breadcrumbs, onion, garlic and parsley together thoroughly with ½ teaspoon salt and plenty of pepper. Use your hands to work the mixture into a firm →

ball – you may need extra breadcrumbs. Divide the mixture into 15–18 little balls, and roll them lightly in flour.

Heat the oil in a frying-pan (skillet). Put in the chicken balls and fry gently for 5-6 minutes, turning to cook evenly. Meanwhile, strain the stock and return it to the saucepan, reserving any bits of chicken and ham from the bones. Bring the stock back to simmering point, and slip in the chicken balls with the oily juices from the frying-pan. Leave them to poach very gently in the stock for 1–2 hours.

Carefully take out the chicken balls and transfer them to a hot serving dish. Scatter in the chopped bits of meat you reserved from the first stock. If there is too much stock, boil it down fiercely, then take it off the heat. To finish, whisk the egg yolk and lemon juice with a little of the hot stock, and then incorporate it into the rest of the stock. Taste and season. Do not reheat, but pour it over the chicken balls immediately.

Serve it with quartered lemons and plenty of bread, Andaluz-style, or plain white rice or mashed potato.

Pollo a la granadina

Chicken with ham and white wine

1½lb/750g chicken joints
4 tablespoons olive oil
1-2 garlic cloves, skinned
and chopped
1 onion, skinned and
chopped
6oz/175g *jamón serrano*
cured ham or raw
gammon, diced
1 large tomato, scalded,
skinned and chopped
1 glass white wine
1 glass water
½ teaspoon grated
nutmeg
1 bay leaf
Salt and pepper

Serves 4

The essential ingredient for any dish designated a la granadina *is the fine ham of Trevelez. During the nineteenth century, every French chef worth his salt included Trevelez ham in his dishes – it was the distinguishing ingredient of* sauce espagnole, *among other dishes. Here it is used to add grandeur to a dish of slow-simmered chicken.*

Cut the chicken joints into small pieces directly across the bone – drumsticks into two pieces, thighs into two, wings into two, breast into four. I do this with a heavy knife tapped through the bone by a sharp blow with a hammer.

Heat the oil in a flameproof earthenware casserole or heavy frying-pan (skillet). Put in the chicken pieces, garlic and onion and cook them gently until they take a little colour. Push to one side and add the diced ham or gammon. Fry for a few moments, then add the tomato and cook it fiercely for 1-2 minutes. Pour in the wine and the water and let it all bubble up again. Add the nutmeg and tuck in the bay leaf.

Turn down the heat, cover loosely and simmer for 30-40 minutes, until the chicken is tender and the sauce well-reduced. Remove the lid and allow the mixture to bubble up and concentrate the juices. Taste and add salt and pepper.

Cordero en ajo cabanil
Lamb with liver and garlic

8 tablespoons olive oil

3lb/1.5kg lamb or kid, including the bone, chopped into bite-sized pieces

4oz/125g lamb's liver, in one piece

1 red pepper, hulled, de-seeded and chopped

2 tablespoons breadcrumbs soaked in a little vinegar and water

1 garlic clove, skinned and roughly chopped

1 tablespoon chopped marjoram or oregano

2 tablespoons *pimentón*

Salt and pepper

Serves 6

This is a party dish usually made with kid – a richer, more glutinous meat than lamb, and the celebration food of Andalucía. I first had this dish at the roofing-out ceremony for my house: the foreman of works was a native of Granada and we ate it off roof-slates.

Heat the oil in a large flameproof earthenware casserole or a heavy frying-pan (skillet). Put in the meat and the liver and fry gently until they are both well browned. Add the chopped pepper and let it take a little colour in the hot oil.

Take out the liver. Test the meat – if it is not yet tender, leave it to simmer until it is. Meanwhile, chop the liver roughly and put it in a blender or food processor with the breadcrumbs, garlic clove, marjoram or oregano, *pimentón*, salt, plenty of freshly milled black pepper and a ladleful of the cooking liquor from the meat. Process to a thick sauce.

As soon as the meat is tender, stir in the sauce. Reheat and simmer gently for another 10 minutes.

Serve hot with bread and a salad of cos lettuce dressed with olive oil, wine vinegar and salt.

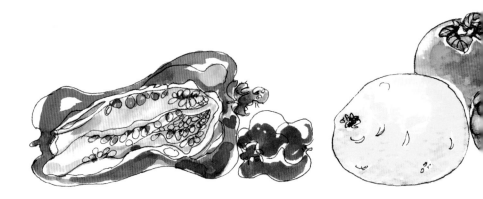

Tocino de cielo

Heavenly bacon

For the caramel
3 tablespoons sugar
2 teaspoons water
Juice of ½ lemon

For the custard
12oz/375g/1½ cups
sugar
A twist of lemon peel
½ pint/300ml/1¼ cups
water
12 large egg yolks

Makes about 10 servings –
it's very rich

The Moors planted sugar cane to satisfy their sweet tooth – the area round Motril produces a fine crop. By the time the Catholic Kings Ferdinand and Isabel finally took Granada and the Moorish occupation was over, the imported taste was centuries old – and old habits die hard. The convents, in particular, continued the tradition and sugary confections made with egg yolks, especially in vine-growing areas, where only the whites are used in wine-clarification, became a speciality of religious festivals. Legend would have it that this particular dish got its name when a nun omitted the egg whites from a sweet she was making and declared the result fit only for pigs.

Make the caramel in an 8 inch/20 cm square baking tin (pan). Melt the ingredients together in the tin, turning it over a high flame until the sugar caramelizes and turns a rich golden brown. Tip to coat the base. Set aside to cool.

To make the custard, put the sugar, lemon peel and water in a heavy saucepan, and heat over a medium flame until the sugar is dissolved. Boil for about 20 minutes. Stir with a wooden spoon until the syrup trails a transparent string when you lift the spoon out. Remove the lemon peel.

Meanwhile, whisk the egg yolks thoroughly. Pour the hot syrup into the eggs, beating as you do so. It will start to thicken. Pour the mixture into the caramel-lined baking tin. Cover with foil. Set the baking tin in the roasting tin and pour boiling water all around. Bake in the oven at 350°F, 180°C, Gas Mark 4 for 30 minutes, until firm.

Allow the custard to cool, then cut it into squares. It is sticky, rich, and as golden as the sunny heavens from which the confection gets its name.

Castañas en almïbar

Chestnuts in syrup

1lb/500g dried chestnuts,
    soaked overnight
8oz/250g/1 cup sugar
2–3 short cinnamon
    sticks

Serves 6

The pigs that forage in the chestnut woods of the Alpujarras have to share their autumn treat with the rest of us: our tastes in wild food are very similar, and a countryman will always take a second look at the roots and fungi his pigs search out. The silky brown nuts are husked and dried to provide a fine winter store. These country cousins of the aristocratic marron glacé are a treat for Christmas.

Put the chestnuts in a large saucepan, cover them with water, bring to the boil and cook them for 10 minutes.

Stir in the sugar and the cinnamon sticks and bring gently back to the boil, stirring until the sugar has dissolved. Turn down the heat, cover loosely and simmer the chestnuts for about 40 minutes, until tender.

Let them cool before serving. They're lovely with sliced oranges and a tiny cup of bitter Moorish coffee.

Soplillos

Almond meringues

This is a speciality of Granada, and just one of a wide range of almond sweetmeats popular all over Andalucía. The most recognizable gastronomic legacy of the Moors, the delicious scent of caramelized sugar and toasted almonds draws children and adults alike into the city's many confiserías each afternoon. When a batch comes out of the oven, a queue quickly forms, and everyone eats happily at the high glass qitunter, *the sticky meringue held in a tiny square of paper. Use the yolks for* Tocino de cielo *(see page 33).*

8oz/250g/1½ cups blanched, toasted almonds
4 egg whites
8oz/250g/1½ cups caster (superfine) sugar
Grated zest of 1 lemon

Makes 20 meringues

Toast the almonds until golden – you can do this in the oven as it heats up to bake the meringues. Pulverize the nuts roughly with a pestle and mortar, or in a food processor.

Whisk the egg whites until they hold soft peaks, and then whisk in the sugar, beating until you have a stiff meringue.

Fold in the grated lemon zest and pulverized almonds. Drop tablespoons of the mixture into paper cases, or onto a baking sheet either lined with rice paper or lightly oiled and dusted with a little flour.

Bake the meringues in the oven at 300°F, 150°C, Gas Mark 2 for 1½ hours. Transfer them to a wire rack to cool.

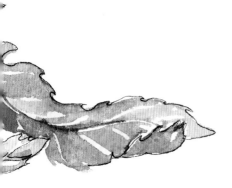

Almería

ALMERÍA, MOST EASTERLY of Andalucía's coastal provinces, was
once a pirate stronghold, and this habit of borrowing with or
without permission from its neighbours dictates her gastronomy.
From the west come the dishes and customs of Granada's
Alpujarras. From the east Almería draws on the culinary traditions
of her Levantine neighbour, Murcia.

The winters here are never hard, so there is always a new crop of
fruit and vegetables in the markets. Date-palms, hedges of
prickly pear and maguey cactus native to the hot plains of
Mexico, give the landscape a feel more of North Africa or
Central America than of Europe. Yet the tawny hills are not as
barren as they seem: the irrigated Andarax valley provides the
province with a market garden which stretches all the way up to
the cave-dwelling Gaudix. The sand and shingle of the littoral
reaches up into a fantastic landscape of red cliffs eroded into

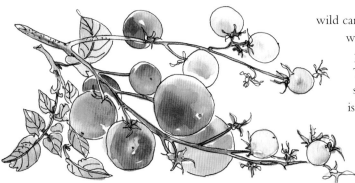

wild canyons that are punctuated with enclosed fertile valleys planted with citrus and vines. The native grape is a large sweet table-grape – and there is a *moscatel* wine made around Purchena. The oranges from the sandy groves of Benahalux and the large-pipped grapes of Ojanes are much esteemed, and exported from the mineral-shipping port of Almería. If there is any particularly Almerían culinary identity, it lies in the generous use of red peppers.

As in the Alpujarras of Granada, the housewives of Almería's hill villages were, since Moorish times, accustomed to earn the extra bit of cash, the corner-of-the-apron money, needed for imported goods such as salt, spices and coffee, by raising silkworms. This home-industry was fuelled by itinerant merchants who both supplied the silkworm eggs and purchased the cocoons, selling them on to the spinners and weavers. Almería itself was famous for its silks. The stuffing went out of the market after the invention of nylon, but the relics of the industry are still traceable in the white-berried mulberry trees (for some reason the worms don't approve of the red-berried species) which still shade *hacienda* courtyards and flourish alongside the ruins of abandoned farmsteads.

The coastal landscape of Almería's province has been transformed over the last decade or so by the introduction of hydroponic cultivation. Acres of glass and plastic now tent the sandy littoral, producing tomatoes, cucumbers, peppers and strawberries for the home and export markets. It is to be hoped that new international regulations will control the use of the chemical fertilizers and pesticides that maintain such artificial environments – the dangers of which are becoming increasingly apparent.

Agua de cebada

Barley water

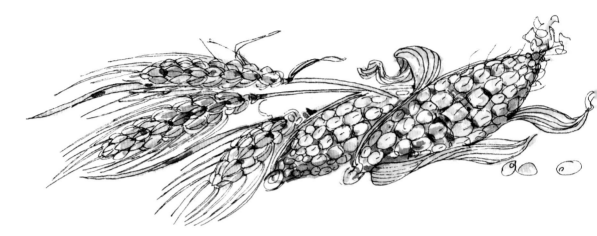

6oz/175g barley, soaked for at least 8 hours or overnight

Grated zest and juice of 1 lemon

3 pints/1.5 litres/7½ cups water

3 tablespoons brown sugar

Makes 3 pints/1.5 litres/ 7½ cups

This is a spill-over from the Levante. Barley is an upland grain – and barley water is as popular as horchata *(nut milk, see page 113) in this region. Make it as thick or as thin as you please by increasing or decreasing the amount of barley. Don't throw the grain away when you have strained it out – it can go into* Sopa de cuarto de hora *(see page 159).*

Drain and rinse the soaked barley and put it in a saucepan with the lemon zest and water – there should be enough water to cover the barley to double its volume.

Bring to the boil and simmer gently for 30 minutes, until the barley is soft. Strain the liquid and return it to the pan. Stir in the sugar, heating gently, until all the granules are dissolved. Stir in the lemon juice. Serve it hot or let it cool and serve with ice and a slice of lemon, diluted as you please.

Ajo colorado con bollos de panizo

Scarlet garlic with cornmeal fritters

For the fritters
10oz/300g/2 cups
   cornmeal (polenta)
1 teaspoon baking soda
1 teaspoon salt
8 floz/250ml/1 cup water
Oil for frying

For the scarlet garlic
1lb/500g potatoes
6 dried red peppers, or
   2 fresh red peppers and
   2 tablespoons *pimentón*
½ onion, skinned and
   chopped
1 garlic clove, skinned
½ teaspoon cumin seeds
Salt and pepper
6 tablespoons olive oil
1 large tomato, scalded,
   skinned and chopped

Serves 4-6

Ajo colorado *is one of the favourite dishes of Murcia, a neighbour of Almería. This version is served with cornmeal fritters – Mexican corn or maize is another of the New World's contributions to the Old World's cooking pot.*

Put the cornmeal in a bowl with the baking soda and salt and stir in the water. Leave it to swell for 2 hours. Meanwhile, make the scarlet garlic. Peel and cut the potatoes into chunks. If you are using dried peppers, de-seed and tear them. If you have fresh peppers, de-seed and slice them.

Put the potatoes, chopped onion and dried peppers (or sliced fresh peppers and *pimentón*) in a saucepan. Pour in enough water to cover. Bring to the boil, turn down the heat, cover and cook the potatoes until tender – about 20 minutes.

Crush the garlic with the cumin and a little salt. Drain the potatoes (save some of the cooking water), and push them through a sieve. Return the potato puree to the pan with the garlic mixture and reheat it gently, beating in the olive oil and chopped tomato. Taste and season – add a little of the reserved cooking water to soften the puree, if necessary.

To finish the fritters, put a deep panful of oil to heat until it will fry a cube of bread golden in an instant. With a bowl of water beside you for moistening your hands, pat-a-cake small balls of dough from palm to palm to make smooth cakes. Drop these into the hot oil, and let them puff up and fry crisp – loosen them from the base of the pan so they float to the top, and baste them with hot oil so they fry evenly. Drain them on kitchen paper, and serve with the scarlet garlic as a dip.

Olla de trigo

Chickpea and wheat soup

1lb/500g chickpeas,
   soaked for a few hours
   or overnight
8oz/250g piece of fat
   bacon
2-3 sprigs fennel, or
   1 teaspoon fennel seeds
8oz/250g whole wheat
Salt and pepper
8oz/250g chorizo or
   other *pimentón* sausage,
   in one piece
1 hot chilli, de-seeded
1 tablespoon *pimentón*
1 slice bread, fried in
   olive oil
8oz/250g morcilla or
   other black pudding,
   sliced

Serves 4-6

Whole wheat grains are included in this winter soup-stew, which makes its pedigree venerable indeed.

Drain the soaked chickpeas. Put them in a large pan with the bacon and fennel and cover with cold water to a depth of two fingers. Bring to the boil, and keep it at a slow boil for 1½ hours, until the chickpeas are soft, adding more boiling water if you need to.

When the chickpeas have been cooking for 30 minutes, put the wheat in a pan and cover it with cold water. Add salt. Bring the water to the boil, turn down the heat and leave it to simmer vigorously for 30-40 minutes, until the grain is tender. Pour the wheat, still simmering, into the chickpea pot. Add the chorizo and bring everything quickly back to the boil. Let it carry on cooking.

Put the chilli, the *pimentón* and the fried bread in a mortar and pound it thoroughly with a pestle, or puree it in a blender or food processor. Stir this mixture into the broth when the chickpeas are soft.

Let it simmer for another 15-20 minutes. Remove and cube the bacon and slice the chorizo, and return them to the pan, along with the sliced morcilla. Taste and season with plenty of salt and pepper.

Serve in deep plates. Some people like theirs with a little vinegar, which is good for the digestion. A neatly skinned prickly pear would make a proper conclusion to the meal.

Migas de maïz de matanza
Cornmeal crumbs with peppers, sausage and grapes

For the migas
1½ pints/900ml/3¾ cups water
1 teaspoon salt
1lb/500g medium-ground cornmeal
4 tablespoons olive oil

For the peppers
1lb/500g green peppers
4-5 tablespoons olive oil
1-2 garlic cloves, skinned and sliced
Sea salt

To serve
Slices of cured meats and sausages, such as *longaniza* (**pimentón sausage**), *lomo* (**cured pork fillet**), and **morcilla (black pudding)**
Sweet white grapes, cucumber chunks, pickled green olives

Serves 4

This is one of that large group of maize-flour porridges which includes Italy's polenta *and Romania's* mamaliga. *This is the meal customarily offered to neighbours who have assisted at the autumn pig-killing. The pan of crisp golden* migas *is set out on the table as it is, flanked by the dish of fried peppers.*

Bring the water and salt to the boil in a wide frying-pan (skillet). Stir in the cornmeal in a steady stream and continue stirring for about 20 minutes until it thickens. As you stir, add the oil, scraping the porridge off the spoon as it sticks. As you work in the oil and the porridge solidifies, dice it roughly with a metal spatula. After a total of 40-45 minutes' hard work, you should have a panful of well-browned cubes of cooked cornmeal. Add extra oil if necessary.

Meanwhile, prepare the peppers. Hull, de-seed and slice them if they are not the thin-fleshed variety. Heat the oil in a frying-pan or saucepan, add the peppers and garlic and cook until soft and brown. Tip them on to a plate with their frying oil. Sprinkle with sea salt and serve with the *migas*.

Set out side dishes of sliced cured meats, sweet white grapes, chunks of cucumber and green olives. Finish with a cup of strong Turkish coffee and an orange.

Arroz a banda

Two-course rice

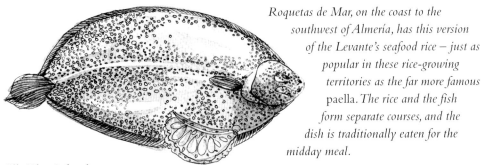

Roquetas de Mar, on the coast to the southwest of Almería, has this version of the Levante's seafood rice – just as popular in these rice-growing territories as the far more famous paella. *The rice and the fish form separate courses, and the dish is traditionally eaten for the midday meal.*

2lb/1kg Arborio
(round-grain) rice
2lb/1kg mixed fish
steaks (firm fish such
as monkfish, tuna and
squid, and soft fish
such as bream, plaice,
lemon sole, coley and
mackerel)
1lb/500g tomatoes
8 tablespoons olive oil
4-5 garlic cloves, skinned
and chopped
1 small onion, skinned
and chopped
2 dried red peppers,
de-seeded and soaked,
or 1 fresh red pepper,
hulled, de-seeded
and chopped (or 2
tablespoons *pimentón*)
8-10 saffron threads,
soaked in a splash
of hot water (or 1
teaspoon ground
saffron)
Salt and pepper
4 pints/2.4 litres/10 cups
water

Serves 6

Pick over the rice and wipe the fish steaks. Cut half the tomatoes in half and grate the flesh, stopping before you reach the skin. Slice the remainder and set aside.

Heat 4 tablespoons of the oil in a shallow flameproof earthenware casserole or heavy frying-pan (skillet) until lightly smoking. Add the garlic, onion and peppers and let it fry for a moment. If using *pimentón*, stir it in off the heat and don't let it fry. Pound or process the fried vegetables with the soaked saffron and its water or the ground saffron thoroughly and return the mixture to the pan. Reheat, stir in the grated tomato pulp and season. Let it all bubble up.

Lay in the firm fish steaks. Pour in the water and bring it back to the boil. Turn down the heat and leave to simmer for 10-15 minutes, depending on the thickness of the steaks. Add the soft fish, reheat and simmer for 5 minutes. Carefully lift out the solid fish and keep it warm. Reserve the stock.

Heat the remaining oil in the rinsed-out pan, add the sliced tomatoes and fry for a few minutes. Pour in the fish stock, bring to the boil, and stir in the rice – two parts fish stock to one part rice. Simmer uncovered, for 15 minutes, stirring constantly. Remove from the heat and leave to swell, loosely covered, for 10 minutes. Serve the rice first, and then the fish.

Escabeche de sardinas

Sardines in aromatic vinegar

1lb/500g fresh sardines
3-4 garlic cloves, skinned
and sliced
2-3 bay leaves
Salt and pepper
2 tablespoons olive oil
2 pints/1.2 litres/5 cups
wine vinegar

Serves 4 as a starter

This is a dish prepared in the fishing villages of the littoral. Almería has its own fishing quarter of La Chanca, named after the net used for catching tuna – its little dwellings, brightly colour-washed and aproned with terraces, are set into the living rock to the west of the city.

Rinse and scale the fish and press lightly on the spine to loosen the flesh. Gut the fish through the soft belly, and then pull the head down through the belly towards the tail, bringing the backbone with it. Sever the bone just below the tail, to give you a butterflied fish.

Arrange a layer of the fish, opened out and skin-side down, in a shallow casserole. Season the layer with garlic slices, bay leaves and salt and pepper. Continue layering until all the fish is used up. Trickle the oil over the top, and pour in the vinegar. Cover with foil.

Bake in the oven at 325°F, 160°C, Gas Mark 3 for about 20 minutes. Remove and set aside the sardines to cool in their juices overnight.

Serve with chunks of coarse bread and a glass of chilled dry white wine.

Salchichas con pimentos colorados
Sausages with red peppers

**1lb/500g all-meat
  sausages**
5 tablespoons olive oil
1 garlic clove, skinned
1 glass dry white wine
1lb/500g red peppers
Salt and pepper

Serves 2

*Red peppers are the most characteristic ingredient in the cooking
of Almería. They are used either fresh, dried, or in powdered form
as the Spanish paprika –* pimentón. *Here, fresh and fried, they
add sparkle to a dish of all-meat sausages. The Spaniard does not
like his sausages bulked out with breadcrumbs.*

Separate the sausages and prick them, so they will not burst.
Warm a tablespoon of the oil with the garlic clove in a
shallow flameproof earthenware casserole or gratin dish.
When the garlic is well browned, remove and discard it.

Put in the sausages and turn them in the hot oil to brown
them all over. Pour in the wine, let it bubble up, then transfer
the casserole to the oven and cook at 350°F, 180°C, Gas Mark
4 for 25-30 minutes, until the sausages are nicely browned but
still moist from the wine.

Meanwhile, roast the peppers over a naked flame until the
skin blisters black. Skin them, then hull, de-seed and cut them
into strips. Dress them with the remaining oil, salt and plenty
of freshly milled black pepper.

Serve the sausages accompanied by the red pepper salad.

Choto con tortas de gachas
Kid in tomato sauce with noodle-dumplings

2 tablespoons olive oil

1 onion and 1 garlic clove,
  skinned and chopped

2 red peppers, hulled,
  de-seeded and sliced

1 tablespoon *pimentón*

3-4 thick streaky bacon
  rashers, and/or
  2oz/50g ham, diced

4oz/125g chorizo

4lb/2kg milk-fed kid or
  shoulder of lamb, cut
  across the bone into
  6-8 pieces

1 glass white wine or dry
  sherry

8-10 saffron threads,
  soaked in a splash of
  hot water

2lb/1kg tomatoes,
  scalded, skinned and
  roughly chopped

Salt and pepper

For the tortas

8oz/250g/2 cups plain
  (all-purpose) flour

½ teaspoon salt

4 tablespoons olive oil

2 tablespoons white wine

6-7 tablespoons water

Serves 6-8

This is a party dish for a big family celebration such as a wedding or first communion. Use partridges, the back legs of a hare or an elderly rabbit, depending on what is available.

Heat the oil in a shallow flameproof casserole and gently fry the onion, garlic and peppers. Stir in the *pimentón*. When the vegetables are soft, push them to one side. Add the bacon and chorizo and let them fry a little.

Add the meat and sauté until it takes a little colour. Splash in the wine or sherry, add the saffron with its water and the tomatoes, and season. Let it all bubble up, then cover and simmer for about 40 minutes, until the meat is tender.

Meanwhile, make the *tortas*. Sift the flour with the salt into a large bowl and make a well in the middle. Put the oil, wine and water into a small pan and heat it to blood temperature. Pour this into the flour, and work the dry and wet ingredients together, first with a wooden spoon and then with floured hands, until you have a smooth, elastic dough (add more liquid or flour as necessary). Let it rest under a cloth for 10 minutes or so, while the flour grains swell. Roll out the dough very thinly on a well-floured board. Cut it into small squares or long thin *tagliatelle*. Dust with flour and set it aside.

When the meat is quite tender, stir the *tortas* into the sauce, adding extra boiling water to submerge them. Simmer for 10-20 minutes, until the *tortas* are soft, or boil the *tortas* separately and stir into the casserole to serve.

Serve with chunks of bread and a salad of tomato and cucumber chunks dressed with mild onion, salt and olive oil.

Dátiles cocidos

Sugared dates

1lb/500g fresh dates
4oz/125g caster
(superfine) sugar

Serves 4–6

Maybe it was the Moors who planted Andalucía's first date-palms. Cultivation in the Middle East goes back at least five thousand years – making it one of the earliest of man's cultivars. Dates have a very high sugar content and were of great importance in the early diet of Arab civilizations, perhaps accounting for the Middle East's highly developed sweet tooth. Fresh dates are yellow and unwrinkled – you need fine, plump fruit with plenty of firm, meaty flesh for this recipe.

Put the dates in a saucepan with enough water to cover them. Bring to the boil and simmer gently for 30–40 minutes. Drain them thoroughly, let them dry in the air, and roll them in plenty of sugar.

If you like, you can take the stone out and replace it with a whole blanched almond or pistachio, or a little rolled 'nut' of marzipan.

Málaga

When some twenty-five years ago I began to spend the summers in southern Spain with my young family, working up to the decision to move the whole outfit permanently to Andalucía, it was near Málaga that I first set up house. I made friends with a local family – impoverished gentry who had their summer house in the hills behind Torremolinos. At the time, the resort was still a little fishing port, just beginning to show the first stirrings of the high-rise jungle it has now become. It was at their hospitable table that I had my first plate of *chunquetes* – tiny transparent spry, the gathering of which is no longer permitted – and *pescaíto frito,* the mixed fried fish which the cooks of Málaga prepare to perfection.

With two children in the pram and one on the way, my kind neighbours recommended a young local girl, niece of their elderly cook, as my maid-of-all-work. Isabel came from Churriana, a little village in the fruit-growing district of the hills inland. Eighteen years old, Isabel was the eldest of six, and as such had helped her mother bring up her siblings; so she was

47

well-used to large families. She stayed with me until I moved out of her province to neighbouring Cádiz, and taught me the simple country dishes common to all Andalucíans. The cookery of Málaga shares much with that of Sevilla, Cádiz, Córdoba and Granada. But it also has its own flavours. Its strengths are the strengths of Andalucía itself, with a bouquet of different gazpachos, rices, and fried fish. Indeed, Málaga's cooks are probably the most talented at that most Andaluz of culinary skills – the preparation of seafood.

Isabel would come back from her visits home with treats for the children. To the little ones, brought up on apples and the fruits of the north, these were strange southern fruits with new and interesting tastes: green figs, medlars, pomegranates and quinces, custard apples and tiny tangerines, prickly pears, carefully de-thorned and peeled to reveal the scarlet flesh under the green skin. And she would bring sweet-scented orange-blossom honey from her father's hives (thick golden nectar packed up in empty fruit-juice bottles), almonds and walnuts still in their furry green shells, wild greens collected from the hillside – thistle-rosettes and bunches of wild asparagus. And she would show the children how to crop the wild, how to suck the vinegar-sharp stalks of the Bermuda buttercup, searching the spring verges for the soft blue-green buds of *Cerinthe major* (*huevos de buey,* or ox-eggs). It was instruction they later put to good use on the way to school.

The local wine is the Málaga *moscatel* – a historic wine much praised in literature – made from vines almost certainly planted by the Phoenicians. Málaga raisins come from wine grapes, sisters under the skin to those of Smyrna whose praises were sung by Homer. The *moscatel* of Málaga is rich and liquoricey, with a warm burnt scent, dark mahogany in colour, sometimes almost black. It is considered more of a lady's tipple – and I love it.

THE FLAVOURS OF ANDALUCÍA

Ajo blanco
Iced almond and garlic soup

The pleasure-loving Moors refined Andalucía's peasant bread soup into this delicate refreshing version of gazpacho: the difference comes from the Moorish-planted almonds and the grapes introduced by the Romans.

Put the bread, almonds, garlic, oil, and two thirds of the water into a blender or food processor and puree. Add the rest of the water until you have the consistency you like. Season with salt and add the vinegar. Leave to infuse in a cold larder or the refrigerator for an hour or so.

Serve the soup in a cup and saucer. Peel and pip the grapes and float them on top of each serving of soup. They will sink or swim – it doesn't matter, as the grapes are more than a garnish, they give the soup its sweet-sharp balance. Place a peeled almond and a little bunch of grapes on each saucer.

Ajo blanco is a good cure for a summer cold – it must be all that garlic.

2-3 slices day-old bread
3oz/75g/½ cup blanched almonds
4 garlic cloves, skinned
2 tablespoons olive oil
1½ pints/900ml/3¾ cups water
Salt
2 tablespoons white wine vinegar

To finish
Peeled almonds
Bunch of small sweet grapes

Serves 4 as a starter

Gazpacho de lujo
Grandee's gazpacho

4oz/125g stale bread
1 pint/600ml/2½ cups
   water
2 tablespoons wine
   vinegar
2lb/1kg ripe tomatoes
1 small cucumber
2 green peppers
1 large Spanish onion
2 garlic cloves, chopped
2 tablespoons olive oil
½ pint/300ml/1¼ cups
   canned tomato juice
Salt

To finish
2 hard-boiled eggs
Croutons fried in olive
   oil

Serves 6

If the many gazpachos of Andalucía are peasant food – there are zoque, gazpachuelo, the cachorrechas of Churriana, porra fria, and a hundred other linguistic variations of the same dish – then this version is the aristocrat of them all, and the one most frequently found in restaurants. Leave out the onion if you are going to keep this in the refrigerator for any length of time as it ferments rather easily. Andaluz families often keep a jug of well-diluted gazpacho handy as a refreshing summer drink. I have given proportions for a thickish mix, but you can suit yourself by adding more water.

Roughly break the bread into pieces and put them to soak in a few tablespoons of the water with the vinegar and the garlic for 10 minutes, while you prepare the vegetables.

Scald and skin the tomatoes and chop them roughly. Chop the cucumber. Hull and de-seed the peppers and roughly chop the flesh. Peel the onion and chop it up. Put aside a quarter of the chopped vegetables in separate dishes, to be handed round separately as a garnish.

Puree the soaked bread and garlic, the rest of the chopped vegetables, and the olive oil. Add the tomato juice and then the rest of the water until you achieve the desired consistency. Adjust the seasoning with salt. Put the soup in a cold larder or the refrigerator for at least 1 hour. Serve as cold as possible (but do not add ice cubes – they taste of the refrigerator and will dilute the soup).

Hand round small bowls of the extra chopped vegetables, hard-boiled eggs and croutons for each person to sprinkle on his own serving.

Cazuela de fideos a la malagueña
Vermicelli with shellfish, prawns (shrimps) and saffron

1lb/500g shellfish such as mussels and/or scallops in the shell (6oz/175g off the shell)
4oz/125g prawns (shrimp)
6-8 saffron threads
3 tablespoons olive oil
1 garlic clove, skinned and sliced
1 Spanish onion, skinned and sliced vertically
1 red pepper, hulled, deseeded and cut into strips
1lb/500g tomatoes, scalded, skinned and chopped
12oz/350g vermicelli
1 tablespoon chopped parsley

Serves 4

Málaga, as all ports, has something of a magpie cuisine, gathering bits and pieces from everywhere. Sailors like to find a taste of home: a dish as well as a girl in every port. Maybe this recipe came in with some merchantman from Naples. Salt cod, bacalao, soaked and torn into pieces, can replace the prawns, and slivered potatoes are sometimes included. If possible, leave the shellfish in plenty of cold water overnight so that they have a chance to spit out their sand.

Put the mussels and/or scallops to soak for a few hours (overnight if possible) in plenty of fresh water. Pick over the prawns (shrimp) and peel them.

Roast and crush the saffron in a spoon held over a flame. Heat the olive oil in a large frying-pan (skillet) and add the garlic, onion and strips of red pepper. Let them fry and take a little colour. Add the saffron and the tomatoes and let the mixture bubble up.

Add the shellfish, turn up the heat, and let the shells open in the steam – no more than 3-4 minutes: they should not over cook. Pour in ½ pint/300 ml/1¼ cups boiling water and bring back to the boil. Stir in the prawns and vermicelli and cook for 1-2 minutes.

Turn the vermicelli and the prawns into the pan with the hot shellfish and sauce. Turn up the heat to evaporate the excess liquid – the finished dish should be juicy but not soupy.

Finish with a sprinkle of parsley. Eat it with a spoon and fork, and a napkin tucked under your chin.

Sardinas en cazuela

Fresh sardine casserole

1½lb/750g fresh sardines
1lb/500g tomatoes,
    scalded and skinned
1 green pepper, hulled
    and de-seeded
1lb/500g onions, skinned
1 garlic clove, skinned
3 tablespoons olive oil
Salt and pepper
1 tablespoon *pimentón*
½ teaspoon ground
    saffron

Serves 4

Alhaurin was the home village of my housekeeper Isabel – and this was her speciality, made with the freshest fish she could find in the market. Sardines, like their cousin the herring, have a layer of rich fat under the skin which makes them ideal for grilling, but too rich for frying. This baked casserole makes the best of oily fish, and is equally good made with fresh herring fillets.

Scale the sardines and butterfly them: press lightly on the backbone, to loosen it, then pull the fish's head sharply down through the soft belly so that the innards and bones come out together. Continue until all the fish are ready. Chop all the vegetables and garlic finely together, to make what is called a *picadillo*.

Trickle a little of the oil in the bottom of an earthenware casserole and spread in a layer of *picadillo*, then a layer of butterflied sardines. Season with the salt, pepper, *pimentón* and saffron. Trickle with oil and spread on another layer of *picadillo*, before adding another layer of sardines. Continue until everything is used up, finishing with a layer of *picadillo*. Cover and cook very gently in the oven, starting at 325°F, 160°C, Gas Mark 3, then, after 10 minutes, turning down to 275°F, 140°C, Gas Mark 1. Cook for about 2 hours, or until the fish is well sauced with its own aromatic oil.

Pescado en blanco
White-cooked fish

1½lb/750g fish, such as
mackerel, small hake
(*pescadilla*), or bream
(the species known as
breca)
1 large potato, peeled and
sliced very thinly, as
for crisps (preferably
sliced on a mandoline)
2 garlic cloves, skinned
and sliced
6 peppercorns, crushed
2–3 parsley sprigs,
chopped
4 tablespoons olive oil
2 pints/1.2 litres/5 cups
water
Juice of 1 lemon
Salt
2oz/50g stale bread,
cubed

Serves 4

This is the simplest everyday way of preparing the fisherman's portion of the catch – that is the fish which would not fetch more than a few pence in the market. It is not a grand recipe, but if it's made with fine fresh fish, it is healthy and good – country cousin to the grand bouillabaisses *of the French littoral. More or less potato goes in depending on how plentiful the catch, and olive oil is used to season and enrich the soup.*

Clean, gut and wipe the fish and chop it into cutlets. (If your fishmonger does this for you, don't forget you need to keep the heads.)

Put the fish, heads and all, into a flameproof casserole with the finely sliced potato, garlic, peppercorns, parsley, olive oil and water.

Bring it slowly to the boil. Allow it one big belch and then stir in the lemon juice and salt.

Sprinkle in the bread cubes, cover and leave to infuse for 20 minutes, then give everything a good stir. Serve with quartered lemons.

Atún mechado
Braised tuna with bacon

2lb/1kg middle cut tunny
   fish
2oz/50g fat green bacon,
   cut into strips
6-8 peppercorns, crushed
4-5 garlic cloves, skinned
   and sliced
1 teaspoon flour
3-4 tablespoons olive oil
1 onion, skinned and
   chopped
1 carrot, scraped and
   chopped
3-4 cloves
1 bay leaf
1 glass dry sherry or
   white wine
1 glass water
Salt and pepper
Bunch flat parsley,
   chopped

Serves 4-6

*Tuna is a much-prized and pretty expensive catch, which means
it makes few appearances in the markets of the littoral, but fetches
a good price in the markets of Madrid. Tuna used to be salted and
conserved for the winter, like salmon and cod, and now we have
tuna-canning factories.*

Take the skin off the fish, then put the flesh in cold water for
30 minutes to soak out the blood. Take it out and pat it dry.
Using a larding needle or a thin sharp knife, insert strips of fat
bacon rolled in the crushed peppercorns, plus a slice of garlic,
into parallel slits along the side of the fish. Dust the fish lightly
with flour. Warm the oil in a frying-pan (skillet) and put in
the tuna, turning it so that it browns a little on all sides.
Transfer to a close-fitting casserole.

Fry the remaining garlic slices with the onion and carrot in
the frying-pan, adding extra oil if necessary, until they soften
and gild a little. Add the cloves, bay leaf, wine and water.

Let it bubble up, season, then tip the contents of the pan into
the casserole. Cover and put the fish to braise gently in the
oven, at 325°F, 160°C, Gas Mark 3, for about 1 hour. Uncover
and cook for another 30 minutes, to brown the fish and
reduce the sauce. Serve with rice or mashed potato, garnished
with parsley.

Pescaíto frito
Fried fishlets

My first lesson in the peculiarly malagueño *skill of frying a bucketful of mixed unidentified spratlings was delivered by my aristocratic neighbour: 'You need a great deal of very hot oil. The fish should pass through only once, and as fast as possible. If bubbles appear on the surface, this is a good sign, as it means the fish are losing their moisture. If no bubbles appear, it means that the oil has soaked into the fish, and the whole procedure has been a failure.' You have been warned.*

1½ lb/750g mixed small fish, such as anchovies, small sardines, sprats or large whitebait, small red mullet, prawns (shrimp), tiny cuttlefish, squid rings, cutlets of larger fish and chunks of monkfish (cheek portions are cheap)
About 6 tablespoons strong unbleached flour
1 teaspoon sea salt
Plenty of oil for frying (a mixture of olive and sunflower is perfect)

Serves 4

Gut the small fish by running your finger down the soft belly. Behead them or not as you please. Sardines will need to be de-scaled first; anchovies won't. Rinse and drain all the fish, keeping them separated according to their species.

Put the flour and salt on a shallow plate. Dust the damp fish with the flour, tossing them lightly with your fingers. You may need extra flour, depending on the size of the fish.

Heat about a finger's depth of oil in a shallow frying-pan (skillet). When the oil is lightly hazed with smoke, drop in the fish, a handful at a time and still in their own groups. Fry the fish until crisp and golden. Remove with a slotted spoon and drain on kitchen paper.

Serve them straight from the frying-pan, still in their different groups, accompanied by lemon quarters. Crisp-fried chips, salted before frying, can make up for any shortfall.

Boquerones en vinagre
Pickled anchovies

1lb/500g fresh anchovies,
small sardines or sprats
2-3 garlic cloves, skinned
and chopped
Salt and freshly milled
black pepper
¼ pint/150ml/⅔ cup
sherry or wine vinegar
4 tablespoons water
1 tablespoon olive oil
1 tablespoon chopped
parsley

Serves 4–6 as a starter

You find these fresh-pickled anchovies in tapa bars up and down the Andalucían littoral. The boquerón is a gregarious fish which moves in great shoals. The Mediterranean sub-species has bright viridian flanks when it is fresh out of the water – a colour that turns to grey-blue and finally nearly black (remember this when choosing the fish). The catch used to be hawked round the streets of Málaga by men and boys carrying baskets suspended from poles across their shoulders. As with all pickled and salted things, they were a way of conserving a plentiful catch for a few more days: fried when fresh, pickled thereafter. Even the mountain pueblos (villages) had their supply of fresh fish. Boys would meet the boats at dawn, load up their donkeys and then race up to the high villages to sell their wares – the first in could ask the best price. The higher up the valley, the less luxurious the fish: sardines and anchovies are the cheapest and most perishable of the fisher-men's catch. Silk cocoons, towering feather-light in their woven grass baskets, were the load for the return journey. But when the invention of nylon knocked the bottom out of the silk trade, the upland pueblos had to wait until the arrival of refrigerated transport before their supplies of fish were fully restored.

Rinse the anchovies – they have no scales to worry about. If you're using sprats or sardines, they will need de-scaling. Gut the little fish by dragging your finger through the soft belly. With the larger fish, pull the head firmly down through the belly towards the tail. This will bring the spine with it and leave the fish split in a butterfly, all in one movement.

Lay all the opened fish flesh-upwards in a shallow dish. Sprinkle with the garlic, salt and pepper. Mix the vinegar with the water and pour it over.

Cover with foil and leave in the refrigerator to marinate for 48 hours. Pour over the olive oil and sprinkle with the parsley. Serve with chunks of bread and a glass of dry sherry.

Espárragos trigeros con migas

Asparagus sprue with breadcrumbs

1lb/500g asparagus sprue
4 tablespoons olive oil
2 slices white bread,
   crumbed
2 tablespoons wine
   vinegar
2 garlic cloves, skinned
   and finely sliced
1 tablespoon *pimentón*
1 glass water
Salt

To finish
1 hard-boiled egg, peeled
   and chopped
1 tablespoon chopped
   parsley

Serves 4 as a starter

Asparagus is a Mediterranean native. Those with sharp eyes can spot the feathery, prickled bushes of the wild variety on the hillsides of Andalucía, at any time of year. But you have to wait for early spring to gather the slender green spears which push up under the protection of the thorns. The Malagueños include asparagus sprue, chopped small, in rice dishes instead of peas.

Rinse and trim the asparagus, and chop it into short lengths. Warm 2 tablespoons of oil in a flameproof earthenware casserole or heavy frying-pan (skillet) and add the bread-crumbs. Let them take up the oil and fry golden. Remove them to a plate and sprinkle with the vinegar.

Fry some of the garlic in the oil that remains in the casserole or pan (you may need a little extra oil). Sprinkle in the *pimentón* and tip the contents of the pan on to the vinegared breadcrumbs. Mash everything together in a pestle and mortar or puree in a blender or food processor, and then dilute the paste with the glass of water.

Fry the last of the garlic in the last of the oil, and add the asparagus. Turn it around in the hot oil, and then pour in the breadcrumb paste. Let it cook gently, uncovered, for about 20 minutes, until the asparagus is tender and the sauce rich and oily. Season with salt.

Finish with a light sprinkling of the chopped hard-boiled egg and parsley.

Cazuela de arroz a la malagueña
Seafood rice

1lb/500g Arborio (round-grain) rice

1lb/500g shellfish, such as mussels and/or scallops in the shell (6oz/175g off the shell), soaked overnight, to spit out their sand

8oz/250g monkfish fillets, cut into large cubes

1 large tomato, halved and grated

4 tablespoons olive oil

1 onion, skinned and chopped

1 green pepper, hulled, de-seeded and chopped

About 2 pints/1.2 litres 5 cups water

1lb/500g raw crayfish or large prawns (shrimp)

Salt

1 teaspoon *pimentón*

1 garlic clove

6 saffron threads (or 1 teaspoon ground saffron)

1 tablespoon chopped parsley

8oz/250g shelled peas

Serves 6

A true paella *is prepared in the open air, traditionally by the father of the family, using the familiar wide, flat double-handled pan over a charcoal fire. This dish, 'a rice' (un arroz), is prepared and cooked by mum in the kitchen at home.*

Heat the oil in a frying-pan (skillet) and sprinkle in the chopped onion and pepper. When the vegetables are soft and gilded, transfer them to a flameproof earthenware casserole. Fry the grated tomato in the remaining oil, and when it has cooked down to a thick juice add it to the vegetables.

Bring a pan of water to the boil, and put in the shellfish. Let them open in the steam (this will take about 4–5 minutes), then remove from the heat. Discard any unopened ones. Split open the rest, saving only the shell with the meat in it. Strain the pan juices into the casserole.

Boil the crayfish or prawns (shrimp) in a saucepan, with water and salt. Leave to cool. Shell the crayfish or prawns and strain the cooking liquid into the casserole.

Pound the *pimentón*, garlic, saffron and parsley with a little salt. Dilute slightly and stir into the casserole.

Bring the casserole to the boil and add the monkfish cubes and peas. Cook for 1–2 minutes. Add the crayfish or prawns and bring back to the boil. Sprinkle in the rice and pour in enough boiling water to submerge the grains.

Bring back to the boil, turn down the heat, and let the rice cook gently, uncovered, for 15–20 minutes, until it is tender. Scatter in the shellfish and remove from the heat. Cover loosely, and leave to swell for 15–20 minutes before serving.

Carne de lidia estofado
Bullring stew

2lb/1kg stewing beef
1 tablespoon salted flour
4 tablespoons olive oil
1 slice fatty bacon or
**   *jamón serrano*, chopped**
1 onion and 2 garlic cloves,
**   skinned and chopped**
1 carrot, scraped and
**   chopped**
1 stick celery, chopped
1 tablespoon *pimentón*
½ teaspoon peppercorns,
**   crushed**
½ bottle red wine
Bouquet garni (rosemary,
**   bay leaf, thyme, mint)**

Serves 4–5

The bullring at Ronda has fair claim to being the cradle of the modern bullfight. However venerable its pedigree, the corrida *or 'running' had a far older and more practical purpose. In the old days, young bulls brought to market were of necessity run through the streets of the town to be penned in the central square, chasing and sometimes catching a few of the less nimble inhabitants as they went. This proved such a popular spectator sport that the* corrida *was formalized into the bullfight. The six bulls still provide the housewives of the town with good cheap meat the morning after – in the past, often the only meat the poor could afford.* Carne de lidia, *the meat from the bullfight, is a little on the tough side, but makes a good stew.*

Cube the meat and roll it in lightly salted flour. Heat the oil in a heavy flameproof casserole and fry the meat over a high heat until it takes a little colour.

Push it to one side, add the bacon or ham, onion, garlic, carrot and celery and cook them gently until they soften and brown. Stir in the *pimentón* and the crushed peppercorns.

Pour in the wine and bubble it up. Add enough water to just submerge the meat, tuck in the *bouquet garni* and bring back to the boil. Sprinkle in a teaspoon of salt.

Cover tightly and leave to simmer very gently either on top of the stove or in the oven at 325°F, 160°C, Gas Mark 3, for 1–2 hours, until the meat is very tender. Check every now and then and add a little more water if necessary.

Serve with rice or mashed potatoes, with a salad of ripe tomatoes and onions to offset the richness of the stew.

Habas a la rondeña

Broad bean casserole

2lb/1kg young broad
   beans in their pods (or
   1½lb/750g podded
   broad beans)
6 tablespoons olive oil
1 onion, skinned and
   chopped
2 garlic cloves, skinned
   and chopped
4oz/125g *jamón serrano*
   cured ham, or
   gammon
2-3 parsley sprigs
1 bay leaf
2 thyme sprigs
1 beef tomato, scalded,
   skinned and chopped
1 small glass dry sherry
   or white wine
1 large glass water
Salt and pepper
Sugar (optional)
1-2 tablespoons fresh
   breadcrumbs
1 tablespoon finely
   chopped parsley
1 tablespoon finely
   chopped oregano or
   marjoram

To finish
4 hard-boiled eggs,
   peeled and quartered

Serves 4-6

Ronda claims this fine stew as her own. I've had it all over the place, but maybe nowhere better than in the restaurant across the way from Ronda's casino, where the old gentlemen play chess and talk of old times. The dish is at its best made when the broad beans are small and tender and the pods, not yet stringy and tough, can be included. I love their sticky, velvety texture – it's rather like okra.

Top and tail the beans, and chop them into short lengths, following the swell of each bean, unless of course you're using podded beans.

Heat the oil in a flameproof earthenware casserole. Put in the onion and garlic and fry for a moment without allowing them to take any colour. Add the ham or gammon, the parsley tied into a little bunch with the bay leaf and thyme, the tomato, sherry or wine and the water. Cover and stew gently for 1-1½ hours, checking and adding extra water if necessary.

When the beans are tender, add salt and pepper, and a little sugar if wished. Cook the stew uncovered for a few minutes to evaporate off all but a rich slick of oily juice. Stir in the breadcrumbs and the finely chopped herbs, to give a little body and texture to the sauce.

Top each serving with quartered hard-boiled eggs. I some-times add the eggs raw, and lightly scramble them with the juices – they go bluey-grey, but taste delicious. This casserole is particularly good with toasted bread rubbed with garlic.

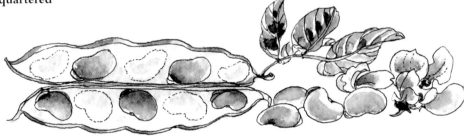

Piriñaca

Liver and lights with wine and herbs

1 lamb's heart, cleaned,
  sliced and blanched
8oz/250g lamb's liver
2 lamb's kidneys,
  trimmed of fat and
  veins
2 tablespoons olive oil
1 onion, skinned and
  finely chopped
1 garlic clove, skinned
  and crushed with a
  little salt
1 small glass Málaga
  moscatel wine
1 glass water
1 teaspoon chopped
  oregano or marjoram
1 teaspoon chopped
  thyme
½ teaspoon crushed
  rosemary
Salt and pepper
1 tablespoon fresh
  breadcrumbs
1 tablespoon chopped
  parsley

Serves 4

*This recipe is from Tolox, a pretty mountain village in the
Serranfa de Ronda much recommended as a spa for respiratory
ailments. This liver and lights dish was prepared after a wild goat
hunt, to stave off the pangs of hunger while the goat itself,
well-seasoned with rosemary and thyme, roasted slowly over a
sage-brush fire. Four or five hours is the recommended cooking
time for a whole goat, so everyone must have been pretty hungry
by the time it was done.*

Check over and slice all the meats finely: they should be in
bite-sized pieces.

Heat the oil in a flameproof earthenware casserole or heavy
frying-pan (skillet) and add the onion and garlic. Let them
cook gently until they soften and gild. Add the meats and
turn them in the hot oil until they brown a little. Pour in the
wine and let it bubble up. Add the water and bring back to
the boil. Stir in the herbs and season with salt and pepper.

Turn down the heat, cover loosely and leave to simmer gently
for about 30 minutes, until the meats are tender. Add extra
water if necessary. Bubble it up again if there is too much
liquid left, and stir in the breadcrumbs and parsley to thicken
and finish the sauce.

Serve with a salad of chopped cos lettuce and cucumber
dressed with lemon juice, salt and olive oil. This is picnic food,
so you will need thick chunks of bread for wiping fingers and
mopping up the sauce.

Caldereta de chivo
Spiced lamb with lemon

1 small shoulder of lamb,
   chopped into steaks
   across the bone
1 teaspoon ground
   cinnamon
½ teaspoon ground
   cloves
½ teaspoon crushed
   peppercorns
1 teaspoon salt
Grated zest and juice of
   ½ lemon
1 small glass olive oil
2 glasses dry white wine
2 bay leaves

Serves 4

This is a dish from Yunquera, high in the mountains east of Ronda. It used to be made with wild goat, the hunter's favourite prey. These stony ranges are lapped with dry scented scrub, and the animals that crop them have sinewy well-flavoured meat which needs long gentle cooking.

Rub the meat with the ground spices, crushed peppercorns, salt, lemon zest and juice. Arrange the pieces in a well-fitting casserole into which you have poured a little of the oil.

Pour the rest of the oil and the wine around the meat. Tuck in the bay leaves. Bake, uncovered, in the oven at 350°F, 180°C, Gas Mark 4 for 1½ hours, basting now and again, until the meat is tender and well browned. You may need to add a little water from time to time to stop the dish from drying out, and lower the heat a notch halfway through the cooking time.

Taste and adjust the seasoning before you serve the meat, sliced, with its own gravy, and a generous helping of mashed potato or plain-cooked rice.

To finish, offer sweet white grapes and a piece of honey-and-almond *turrón* (nougat), the Spanish *halva*, a legacy of the Moorish occupation.

Pan de pollo
Chicken loaf

1 small chicken
8oz/250g pig's liver
8oz/250g pork belly
1 glass sherry or white
    wine
1 tablespoon chopped
    parsley
Pepper
1 tablespoon pork-lard
1 tablespoon chopped
    onion
1 garlic clove, skinned
    and chopped
1 egg, lightly beaten
2 tablespoons
    breadcrumbs
1 bay leaf

Serves 6

A peasant community is careful with its stores. A chicken was not sacrificed lightly to the pot: eggs are too valuable a source of protein. So, in rural communities, chicken dishes are for special occasions, including carnival time, that period of feasting and license celebrated just before the long Lent fast.

Strip the meat from the raw chicken, keeping the breast fillets separate. Keep the skin whole, if you can, so that you can wrap the pâté in it (start with a long cut down the back).

Mince the liver, pork and dark chicken meat together, mix in the sherry or white wine, parsley and plenty of pepper. Melt some lard in a frying-pan (skillet), add the onion and the garlic and fry gently. Mix them with the minced meats, beaten egg and breadcrumbs, to make a smooth stuffing paste.

Lay the chicken skin, if whole, in a greased roasting tin (pan), or thoroughly grease a deep earthenware dish with the rest of the lard, and lay on half the stuffing mixture in a flattened sausage shape. Place the breast fillets on top, and cover with the rest of the stuffing. Place a bay leaf on the top and wrap in greased foil.

Cook in the oven at 350°F, 180°C, Gas Mark 4 for 1-1½ hours, until the juices run clear when a skewer is pushed into the middle.

Serve it warm, or, if you want to serve it cold, leave it under a weight overnight in a cool place.

Pepitoria de pollo
Chicken with almonds

2lb/1kg chicken joints
4 tablespoons olive oil
1 thick slice day-old
 bread, broken into
 pieces
2 garlic cloves, skinned
 and chopped
Small bunch parsley
1 tablespoon ground
 almonds
½ teaspoon ground
 cloves
1 teaspoon ground
 cinnamon
6 saffron threads soaked
 in a splash of boiling
 water (or 1 teaspoon
 ground saffron)
Grated zest and juice of
 1 lemon
1 glass sherry or white
 wine
1 onion, skinned and
 finely chopped

Serves 4–5

Almonds remain an important cash-crop for the small farmers of Málaga's province: trees are usually planted on a slope so that the nuts will roll down the incline and camino real, which provisioned the flocks travelling across Spain, are anyone's crop. I remember, one bright autumn day in the hills, coming across an old farmer collecting the crop from trees which formed a bridal arch over the narrow road. He filled the children's pockets and my hands with warm brown nuts and grinned at us: 'Take them – they're free. Be glad our fathers planted them for us to gather.'

Chop the chicken joints in half – the easiest way is with a hammer and a heavy knife.

Heat the oil in a frying-pan (skillet). Add the bread and the garlic and fry until golden, then toss in the parsley sprigs. Transfer the contents of the pan to a food processor or a mortar. Add the ground almonds, spices, saffron, lemon zest and juice, and sherry or wine and process or pound with a pestle to a thick sauce.

Gently fry the chicken pieces and the onion in the oil that remains in the pan (you may need to add more oil). When the chicken is lightly browned and the onions are soft, stir in the sauce. Bring to the boil, then cover and turn down the heat. Simmer gently for 20–30 minutes, until the chicken is quite cooked, adding more water if the sauce dries up.

Serve with chips and a salad.

Patatas en ajopollo
Potatoes with almonds and saffron

2lb/1kg potatoes
6–8 saffron threads
4 tablespoons olive oil
2oz/50g/½ cup blanched
   slivered almonds
1 garlic clove, skinned
   and sliced
1 slice stale bread, cubed
Salt and pepper

Serves 4

The use of a single heat source and one pot is one of the most ancient ways of preparing food. The technique of cooking an oil-enriched stew right down until it fries in its own juices is applied here to a New World import, the potato.

Peel the potatoes and cut into chunks. Put them into a wide saucepan and cover with salted water. Roast the saffron threads in a spoon held over a flame and tip them in with the potatoes.

Warm the oil in a small frying-pan (skillet), sprinkle in the almonds, garlic and bread. Fry them all until golden. Transfer the contents of the frying-pan to a blender, food processor or pestle and mortar. Crush them all together with a little water, tip in with the potatoes and season.

Bring to the boil, turn down the heat and simmer the potatoes loosely covered, until nearly tender. Take off the lid and bubble up to evaporate all the liquid, until they are frying in their own juices. Let them brown a little before serving, piping hot.

Borrachuelos
Drunken biscuits

Orange-flavoured and bathed in honey, these are a party food and have to be made in quantity. Fritters – of which the yeast-raised variety is the doughnut, and the northern version is the pancake – pop up at carnival time all over Europe.

Heat the olive oil with the piece of orange peel to take away the oily flavour. When it boils, take it off the heat, and put it aside to cool.

8 floz/250ml/1 cup olive oil
A strip of orange peel
1 tablespoon sesame seeds
1 tablespoon fennel seeds
4 floz/100ml/½ cup Málaga *moscatel* wine
4 floz/100ml/½ cup dry sherry
Juice of 1 orange and 1 lemon
12oz/350g/3 cups plain (all-purpose) flour
Oil for frying

To finish
1lb/500g honey
Icing sugar

Makes about 30 biscuits

When it is just warm, stir in the sesame and fennel seeds and pour the mixture into a large bowl with the wine, sherry and fruit juices. Sieve in the flour, working it in gradually with a wooden spoon until you have a smooth dough (this can be done in a food processor).

Put the dough on to a well-floured board and knead it thoroughly, working in extra flour if you need it. Break off walnut-sized pieces and roll out each piece to a diameter of about 2 inches/5 cm across. Or you can roll out the whole piece and cut out disks with a wineglass.

Heat the frying oil until it is lightly hazed with smoke. Slip in the biscuits one by one, and fry them until golden. Lift them out carefully with a slotted spoon, and transfer them to a dish lined with kitchen paper. Leave them overnight. The next day, melt the honey with a little water in a saucepan over a high heat. Dunk the biscuits in the hot syrup, then put them to drip on a rack. When they are cool, dust with icing sugar and serve.

Melocotón en almïbar

Peaches in syrup with vanilla

4 large yellow peaches
6oz/175g/¾ cup sugar
A curl of orange peel
1 short vanilla pod
1½ pints/900ml/3¾ cups
  water

Serves 4

Andalucía produces big firm yellow peaches which can stand up to the fierce summer sun. Even when fresh peaches are in season, peaches in syrup are the most popular dessert.

Scald the peaches with boiling water and slip off their skins. Put the sugar, orange peel and vanilla pod in a large saucepan, cover with the water and bring to the boil, stirring to dissolve the sugar.

Slip in the peaches, bring the syrup back to the boil, and poach the fruit gently for 10-15 minutes, depending on their size. Let the peaches cool in their syrup.

These peaches are lovely served with vanilla ice cream and the *Borrachuelos* on page 66.

Peras estofadas
Pears with honey and cinnamon

8 small firm pears
Grated zest and juice of
   1 lemon
1 short cinnamon stick
8oz/250g honey
1 small glass sweet wine
About 1 pint/600ml
   2½ cups water

To finish
8 toasted almonds

Serves 4

The fertile valley of the Guadalhorce, watered all year from the springs in the mountains behind, produces marvellous fruit. Spain has few postres *(desserts) because her fruit dish is so well-laden, and meals can so easily be concluded with a bunch of sweet grapes, a juicy orange, or a ripe fig. However, the Moors were not always content to let nature lie unadorned, and some of their culinary habits lingered long after they took ship from Málaga's shores.*

Peel the pears, leaving the stalks in place, and set them, stalk heavenwards, in a saucepan just large enough to accommodate them. Sprinkle them with the lemon juice.

Put the lemon zest, cinnamon stick, honey, wine and water in another pan. Bring to the boil, stirring to dissolve the honey. Turn down the heat and simmer for 5 minutes.

Pour the boiling syrup over the pears in the other saucepan – you may need more boiling water if there isn't enough to cover the fruit. Bring the syrup back to the boil and immediately remove the pan from the heat. Allow the pears to cool in the syrup.

Carefully transfer the pears and their syrup to a pretty glass dish. Replace each stalk with a toasted almond, and serve.

Uvas en anïs

Grapes in anisette

1lb/500g small sweet
    grapes
1 bottle anisette
    (aguardiente), or vodka
    with 1 teaspoon of
    aniseeds added

*Makes a 1¾ pint/
    1 litre/4½ cup jar*

This is an Andalucían New Year treat – you have to eat one grape for every stroke of midnight if you want good luck in the year to come. What you get, of course, is indigestion and a hangover. And the way to put that right is an egg yolk whipped up with a little of the grape liquor from the night before. This recipe is made with the last grapes of autumn.

Scald a Kilner jar. Snip the grapes neatly off their stalks, leaving a scrap of stalk behind to act as a plug.

Pack the grapes in the Kilner jar and pour in the spirit. Seal and leave for 2-3 months, until it's time to welcome in the next New Year.

Cádiz

CÁDIZ, MY HOME TERRITORY, is Andalucía's southernmost province, its earth scorched by the hot breath of Africa. It guards the gates through which the Mediterranean gains access to the Atlantic, and its harbours have accommodated many visitors: Phoenicians and Greeks, the warriors of Carthage and Rome, Vikings, Turks and Moors – all left their mark on the landscape and people. My local port of Tarifa, at the very tip of Europe, gave its name to the taxes now imposed by the world's customs posts.

Partly because it has had so many visitors, but also because it is blessed with a fine geography – a long coastline giving access to the fishing grounds of the Atlantic and the Mediterranean, a littoral of farmland and market gardens, all backed with mountain and forest to shelter wild game and allow free range for the black

cattle and lean red pigs which make the best hams – Cádiz has some of the best food in all Andalucía. Add to all this Roman-planted olive groves and the most ancient vineyards in all Iberia producing the straw-pale dry sherry-wines of Jérez and Sanlúcar, and the province seems unsurpassable for gastronomic pleasure.

But then, perhaps I'm prejudiced. In defence of my recommendation, I can only say that I could walk into any bar from Algeciras to Cádiz and have a plate of the freshest and most delicate seafood frittered to perfection in the thick green-gold olive oil of Dos Hermanas, continue with a bowl of the best of slow-simmered vegetable-and-ham-enriched stews, and finish with a handful of the fine, plump, green honey-sweet figs of Jérez. And I can then walk down a sunlit street, under a glossy green canopy of orange trees, for a cup of dense black coffee and one of those rich sugar-almond confections that the Moors left as a permanent reminder of seven centuries of Islamic civilization.

The salt flats of Cádiz which once supplied the ancient world with its most valuable commodity are still in full production. The rough grains add a sparkle to a crisp salad, a fine flavour to the juicy grilled prawns that are a speciality of the seaside bars, a sharp crunch to the frying batter. When I lived not far down the coast from Cádiz, I would make an autumn trip with a wooden drawer to collect enough rough grey salt from the sparkling pyramids by the roadside to cure the bacon from our household pig.

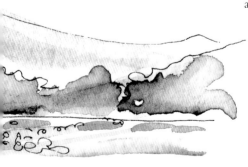

A few of the more isolated communities mill their own flour and bake their own bread. It's usually the women who are the bakers, a skill passed from mother to daughter, along with a cupful of the soured dough whose yeast-culture might go back for decades. The Romans praised the good bread of Andalucía; it is solid food – *pan macho,* 'masculine bread', unbleached and containing the germ, and fortified with a speck of lime to strengthen bones and teeth. Add to all this, fruit and vegetables from the market gardens of Rota, and I feel my case is argued.

Conchas finas a la sanluqueña
Cockles with manzanilla

2 pints/1.2 litres live cockles, mussels or any bi-valve you please
2 tablespoons olive oil
2 garlic cloves, skinned and sliced
1 generous glass manzanilla or other dry sherry
4 tablespoons chopped parsley
Grated zest of ½ lemon

Serves 4 as a starter

The inhabitants of the small port of Sanlúcar gather a particularly delicious small bi-valve which flourishes in the soft grey mud of the Guadalquivir's estuary. With the exception of rope-grown mussels, all bi-valves need a thorough rinsing in fresh water to get rid of their grit, mud and sand.

Rinse the shellfish, checking over and discarding any which are broken or gape open or whose weight betrays that they are full of sand.

Put the oil to warm in a wide frying-pan (skillet) – you need a good spread of heat. When it is lightly hazed with smoke, toss in the garlic and fry for a moment. Pour in the sherry. Turn up the heat, add the shellfish, cover and shake the pan so that the shells open in the steam (this will take only a few minutes). Add the parsley and lemon zest, and serve the cockles immediately in deep bowls, with their liquor.

Reheating shellfish toughens it – so add leftovers to a seafood cocktail, or a potato salad dressed with plenty of spring onion, sherry vinegar and olive oil.

Caldillo de perro
Fish soup with bitter orange

**2lb/1kg whole small hake
   or codling**
Salt
8 tablespoons olive oil
2-3 garlic cloves, skinned
**1 large Spanish onion,
   skinned and finely
   chopped**
**Juice of 1 bitter orange –
   or a mixture of orange
   and lemon juice**

To finish (optional)
**Rounds of bread dried
   crisp in the oven**

Serves 3-4

This fish soup is a very ancient dish indeed. No Crusader spices or New World imports mar its pedigree. The flavours are subtle: a little sharp and salty, sweet and sour. Variations on the theme are to be found in fishermen's bars right round the littoral, wherever the Phoenicians once cast anchor. This particular version is a speciality of the tavernas of Cádiz and Puerto de Santa Maria. *The fish used is the* merluza pescadilla, *young hake, which should be so fresh it slips straight from the net into the pot, though fresh codling may be substituted.*

Cut the fish into thick steaks, including the head. Salt it well and leave it to stiffen for 1 hour.

Meanwhile, warm the oil with the garlic cloves in a heavy flameproof earthenware casserole or saucepan. Let the oil take the flavour of the garlic; remove and discard the cloves when they turn gold. Stir in the onion and let it soften in the hot oil. Just before it begins to take colour, pour in a cupful of boiling water. Bring everything back to the boil, put the lid on and leave to bubble along very gently for an hour or so, until the onion is mushy. Add another cup of water, bring it all back to the boil, and slip in the fish steaks, one at a time, taking care to bring the broth immediately back to the boil.

Put the lid back on and let the fish boil fiercely, until it is very soft (15 minutes is enough). Take the soup off the heat and stir in the bitter orange or orange-and-lemon juice.

Serve the soup piping hot in its earthenware casserole, with slices of dried bread to crumble in, if wished.

Gambas a la parilla
Salt-grilled prawns

1lb/500g fresh unpeeled raw prawns (shrimp)
1-2 tablespoons olive oil
1-2 tablespoons rough sea salt (the chunkier the better)

Serves 4 as a starter

Rough salt from the salt flats of Cádiz and perfectly fresh raw prawns are the only secret to this simple dish. The housewives of Tarifa are particular about their crustaceans, and will thrust an enquiring finger into the whiskery mass and lick the juice to see if the haul has been brined – a sure sign that the shrimp or prawn has been over-long in the trawler's hold.

Brush the prawns (shrimp) with oil and sprinkle them with the rough salt – this stops them sticking to the griddle and gives a lovely caramelized shell.

Heat a griddle or heavy frying-pan (skillet). In Spain, cookers are fitted with a built-in griddle, an iron or steel plate with the heat source directly beneath – perfect for searing fillets of meat or fish as well as opening shellfish and grilling crustaceans.

When the griddle or pan is smoking hot, lay on the prawns neatly tucked spoon-fashion one behind the other. Depending on the size, cook for 2-4 minutes, no more, turning them once.

Serve with quartered lemons and plenty of bread for wiping fishy fingers.

Gambas pil-pil
Prawns (shrimps) in olive oil with garlic

A sizzling little casserole of scarlet-veined prawns, sweet and firm in their aromatic bath of olive oil, was the most expensive delicacy my local tapa bar in Tarifa could offer. Pil pil (cooked in an earthenware casserole) – a term also applied to the northern delicacy of kokochas (hake throats) – is held by some to be onomatopoeic, suggesting the noise made as the juices stutter and spit. But there are as many theories as there are bubbles in boiling oil: to me the name sounds as Moorish as the arches that pierce the ramparts of Tarifa.

You really do need uncooked unfrozen prawns (shrimp) for this simple dish – ready-cooked frozen ones have a cotton-wool texture which absorbs too much oil. Peeling raw prawns is a fiddly job, but well worth the delicious results.

¼ pint/150ml/1⅔ cup
  olive oil
2-3 garlic cloves, skinned
  and sliced
12oz/350g fresh raw
  prawns (shrimp),
  peeled
4 small dried chillies,
  de-seeded and torn
  into pieces
Salt

Serves 4 as a starter

Divide the oil between 4 small shallow casseroles. Put them to heat either on the top of the stove if they are flameproof or in a very hot oven. When the oil is sizzling, add the garlic.

Drop in the prawns (shrimp) and the pieces of chilli. Bring everything back to the boil, adding more oil if the prawns absorb it all.

As soon as the oil is spitting-hot, serve the prawns in their small cooking dishes – either tapa bar-style with small wooden forks or with wooden cocktail sticks so you do not burn your mouth. Provide plenty of bread for mopping up the aromatic oil.

Pinchitos moruños

Moorish kebabs

1lb/500g boneless pork or lamb (heart or kidney can be used instead)
2 tablespoons olive oil
1 teaspoon whole cumin seeds
½ teaspoon chilli powder
1 teaspoon ground coriander
1 teaspoon ground turmeric
1 teaspoon ground white pepper
12 slender skewers or steel knitting needles
1 teaspoon salt

To finish
12 bread chunks

Serves 4 as a starter

Pinchitos *(little thorns) are the great festival fairground treat of southern Spain. A skewerful (often a fine steel knitting needle which you are honour-bound to return) of tiny pieces of meat, marinated in a mixture of Moorish spices, are deftly turned over a small oblong brazier of glowing coals, each to order, by a 'Moor' in a scarlet fez. The scent of the fire-roasted meat curls up the streets, drawing the crowds to the fairground as seductively as the flashing lights and booming music.*

Cut the meat into small cubes and mix it together with the oil, spices and pepper. Leave it in a cool place to absorb the flavours. Thread the cubes of meat on to the skewers – 10-12 pieces on each. Heat the grill (broiler) or barbecue. Grill (broil) the kebabs over a very high heat, turning them frequently, until well browned but still juicy.

Sprinkle them with salt just before you take them off the heat. Serve the meat on the skewers, with a chunk of bread speared on the end of each skewer.

Tortillitas de camarones
Shrimp fritters

3 eggs
3 tablespoons water
3 tablespoons chickpea
    flour
1 tablespoon chopped
    parsley
1 tablespoon grated
    onion
1 tablespoon *pimentón*
Salt and pepper
6oz/175g tiny unpeeled
    raw shrimp
Oil for frying

Serves 4 as a starter

The cooks of Cádiz fry better than anyone else in Spain. It's a skill bred in the bone and has to do with an instinct for the perfect tempering of the saltén – the thin iron frying-pan (skillet) which is very sensitive to direct heat – the exact temperature to which to heat the olive oil, and the precise thickness of the batter. These fritters are made with tiny unpeeled shrimps – they jump like fleas and turn opaque white when cooked – which are caught by the bucketful along the sandy beaches of Cádiz's shining Coast of Light.

Beat the eggs and water lightly together. Work in the flour, beating to avoid lumps. Leave it to rest for 30 minutes, so that the flour swells. Beat in the parsley, onion and *pimentón*, then season. Toss in the shrimps, shells and all.

Heat two-fingers' depth of oil in a frying-pan. When it is lightly hazed with smoke, drop in tablespoons of the batter mixture – not too many at once or the oil temperature will drop. Fry the fritters crisp and golden brown, turning them once. Put them to drain on kitchen paper and serve them straight away, with lemon quarters and a glass of cold dry sherry to cool your tongue.

Ostiones gratinados

Oysters au gratin

12 oysters on the half shell

2–3 garlic cloves, skinned and finely chopped

4 tablespoons finely chopped parsley

4 tablespoons fresh breadcrumbs

1 small glass anis or Pernod (optional)

Olive oil

Serves 4 as a starter

The ostion is an elongated oyster similar (some authorities say identical) to the Portuguese oyster, but rougher and more strongly flavoured than those from the rocks of the north, so that it is not very palatable raw.

Arrange the oysters in the grill (broiler) pan. Mix the chopped garlic, parsley and breadrumbs. Add a drop of anis or Pernod, if you are using it, to each oyster. Top each oyster with a little hat of the breadcrumb mixture. Trickle olive oil over the top.

Pop the oysters under a very hot grill for 2–3 minutes until the topping is crisp and brown. Serve immediately with quartered lemons.

Sopa de cuarto de hora con ostiones y calamares
Fifteen-minute soup with oysters and squid

There are many variations of these quick and easy soups which can be thrown together to stave off the pangs of hunger while the main dish is cooking. This version is from Puerto Real. Oysters need only quick poaching, so this is a fine way to make the most of a few of these prized shellfish. Mussels or small scallops make a good substitute.

12 oysters
8oz/250g squid
1½ pints/900ml/3¾ cups
    water
2oz/50g vermicelli
1 tablespoon olive oil
2 tablespoons chopped
    parsley
4oz/125g chopped *jamón
    serrano* cured ham, or
    lean bacon
1 small glass manzanilla
    or other dry sherry
Salt and pepper

To finish
2 hard-boiled eggs,
    peeled and chopped

Serves 4

Open the oysters (a few hours in the freezer does the trick if you cannot manage an oyster knife). Save the juices and reserve the fish.

Clean the squid, pull out the clear 'plastic' bone and scoop out the insides. Trim off the stomach and eyes (the top section of the body) and scrape off the little fingernails on the tentacles. Give it all a good rinse – cephalopods hang around in shallow sandy water. Slice the body and tentacles into small pieces.

Put the oyster juices into a saucepan with all the ingredients except the oysters and hard-boiled eggs. Bring to the boil and simmer for 10 minutes, then slip in the oysters and poach them for 1 minute.

Stir in the chopped hard-boiled egg. Serve the soup as soon as it's ready, with quartered lemons.

Atún con pimentón

Fresh tuna with pimentón

**2lb/1kg thick-cut tuna
steaks**
4 garlic cloves, skinned
1 teaspoon salt
2 tablespoons *pimentón*
8 tablespoons olive oil
**2 tablespoons sherry or
wine vinegar**
2 bay leaves
1 lemon, finely sliced

Serves 6

*The Phoenicians caught tuna off the coast of Cádiz; the Romans
salted it and shipped it back to their capital. The migrating shoals
of tuna, abundant until depleted by recent over-fishing and
pollution, provided the fishermen of Cádiz with a bi-annual
bonanza. There are now disused tuna-salting stations all round
the Mediterranean coast and the noble tunafish has become a rare
prize. Make this dish with skate or monkfish if you can't find
fresh tuna.*

Wipe the tuna steaks and lay them in a casserole. Crush the
garlic with the salt and *pimentón* and mix it with the oil and
sherry or wine vinegar.

Pour the aromatic oil over the tuna, tuck in the bay leaves and
lay the lemon slices over the top. Put on the lid or cover with
foil and bake in the oven at 425°F, 220°C, Gas Mark 7 for
20–30 minutes, until the fish is cooked through. You can cook
it gently on top of the stove if you prefer, but make sure the
casserole is flameproof.

The pink fish coated with scarlet sauce and decorated with
lemon makes a very attractive dish. Serve it warm with
quartered lemons, red peppers fried with oil and garlic, and a
crisp green salad.

Urta con dos salsas

Sea bream with two sauces

**4 thick sea bream, hake,
halibut, turbot,
or cod fillets**
1 tablespoon oil
**1 heaped tablespoon
seasoned flour**
Salt

For the **picadillo**
**1 beef tomato, scalded,
skinned and finely
chopped**
**½ mild Spanish onion,
skinned and finely
chopped**
**½ green pepper, finely
chopped**
**½ red pepper, finely
chopped**
**1 tablespoon finely
chopped parsley**
4 tablespoons olive oil
**1 tablespoon sherry
vinegar**

For the **allioli**
1 egg yolk
**1-2 garlic cloves, skinned
and finely chopped**
½ teaspoon salt
**¼ pint/150ml/⅔ cup
olive oil**
**1 tablespoon sherry
vinegar**

Serves 4

Those who fish between the Pillars of Hercules claim the urta, *a
particularly handsome species of sea bream, is found nowhere else.
This is how the Meson Sancho, my local bar-restaurant when I
lived with my family in the hills overlooking the Straits, prepared
the firm-flaked, snow-white fillets.*

Salt the fish fillets. Make the sauces. The *picadillo* (chopped
sauce) needs only to be mixed and marinated for 30 minutes.
The *allioli* is made like a mayonnaise. See that all the ingredients are at room temperature. Work the yolk with the finely
chopped garlic and salt – when the quantity is small, as here,
use a fork and a soup plate. Fork in the oil, dribble by dribble,
until you have a lovely thick shiny sauce. If the yolk is on the
small side, it will not accept all the oil, so go easy and watch
out for splitting. In the unlucky event of it splitting, add a
drop of boiling water and work outwards. Alternatively, work
the split sauce, blob by blob, into a spoonful of mild mustard.

Heat a griddle or iron frying-pan (skillet) until it is smoking
hot. Brush the fish fillets lightly with oil and dust them with
flour. Place the fish on the griddle or in the frying-pan and
let it sizzle, turning once, until the outside is deliciously
blistered and crisp, and the inside still moist and juicy.

Serve the fish flanked by a spoonful of each of the
two sauces.

Boronia de Rota

Pumpkin and marrow casserole

1lb/500g pumpkin,
   peeled, de-seeded and
   cut into chunks
1lb/500g marrow, peeled
   if necessary, de-seeded
   and cut into chunks
1lb/500g quinces or sour
   apples, peeled, cored
   and cut into segments
1 small glass sherry or
   wine vinegar
1 tablespoon brown sugar
¼ pint/150ml/⅔ cup
   olive oil
1 large Spanish onion,
   skinned and finely
   chopped
1lb/500g green peppers,
   hulled, de-seeded and
   cut into strips
1lb/500g aubergines
   (eggplants), hulled and
   diced
2lb/1kg tomatoes,
   scalded, skinned and
   chopped
1 teaspoon chopped
   oregano or marjoram
Salt and pepper

Serves 6

The port of Rota has been famous for its vegetables ever since it introduced New World pumpkins and marrows to Andalucía's winter store cupboard. So well did the pumpkins flourish that Napoleon's troops, advancing to storm and sack the city, mistook the monster globes for the mouths of cannon and withdrew in search of easier prey.

Put the chunks of pumpkin, marrow and quince into a roomy saucepan, add the vinegar, sugar and enough water to come two thirds of the way up the vegetables. Bring to the boil, cover and simmer for 20-30 minutes, until the vegetables are soft. (If you are using apples rather than quinces, add them halfway through.) Uncover, and boil the juices fiercely for a few moments to evaporate off the excess water.

Meanwhile, warm the oil in a large frying-pan (skillet) and fry the onion and strips of pepper gently, until they soften and gild. Drain in a sieve over a bowl and pour the drippings back into the pan. Add the aubergine (eggplant) and fry until it too is soft and lightly caramelized. Add the tomato and let it all bubble up to make a thick sauce. Stir the onion and the green peppers back in, add the herbs, and season. Tip the sauce into the cooked vegetables and mix everything together. Let it simmer gently for a few minutes. Serve with bread and cheese to complete the meal.

Tortilla de esparrágos strigueros

Asparagus omelette

8oz/250g asparagus
   sprue
4 eggs
Salt and pepper
2 tablespoons olive oil

Serves 4 as a starter, 2 as a
main course

The first gastronomic pleasure of the Andalucían spring comes in the form of the spindly stalks of wild asparagus which shoot up beneath the protection of the thorny tangle of last year's growth. Gypsy children gather them for market, and offer bundles neatly tied with grass-stalks and labelled either 'bitter' or 'sweet' – the bitter being considered a good addition to a chickpea stew, and the sweet ones best for a tortilla. We soon learnt how to recognize the bushes, and gathered our own supplies.

Chop the slender stalks of asparagus sprue into short lengths. Put them in a colander and blanch them by pouring boiling water over them.

Fork the eggs with the salt and pepper – not too vigorously as the white and yolk should remain a little streaky. Stir in the blanched asparagus.

Heat the oil in a small omelette pan. Tip in the egg mixture. Cook the omelette as you would a thick pancake, forking it up at first to allow the top egg to run underneath and set. Tap in the sides to build up an edge. As soon as it is softly set, turn the tortilla out on to a plate and then slide it back into the pan to cook the other side. Serve immediately.

Champiñones al ajillo
Mushrooms with garlic

1lb/500g large, flat, black-
    gilled mushrooms
4-5 tablespoons olive oil
2 garlic cloves, skinned
    and finely sliced
1 tablespoon chopped
    oregano
Salt and pepper
1 glass dry sherry
2 tablespoons
    breadcrumbs
2 tablespoons chopped
    parsley

*Serves 4 as a starter, 2 as a
    main course*

Although Andalucía does not think much of its indigenous fungi crop – perhaps because spores of African species make identification doubly difficult – the gypsies gather field mushrooms for sale in the autumn. We learned that the best crops were to be gathered among the charred shrubs and blackened earth left in the wake of the autumn's forest fires. The flavour of the big, flat, black-gilled mature caps is so good it needs no embellishment.

Shake any beasties out of the mushrooms. Wipe them, but do not peel or wash them. Trim off the stalks close to the base.

Heat the oil in a shallow flameproof earthenware casserole or a wide frying-pan (skillet), toss in the garlic and arrange the mushrooms in a single layer. Sprinkle with oregano, salt and plenty of black pepper. Fry the mushrooms gently until the juice runs. Turn them over and fry the other side.

Remove the mushrooms and splash in the sherry. Let it bubble up to evaporate the alcohol, and then stir in the breadcrumbs and parsley to absorb the juices. Top the mushrooms with the aromatized breadcrumbs.

Serve piping hot – give them a final blast under the grill (broiler) if you like.

Alcauciles fritos

Fried baby artichokes

**6-8 small artichokes,
 with their stems**
Lemon juice
Sea salt
Oil for frying

Serves 2 as a starter

Bouquets of tiny purple artichokes garland the vegetable stalls of Andalucía's markets in early summer, and the best come from the vegetable gardens of the seaside dunes. These small artichokes are not baby versions of the large ones, but a variety grown specially for deep-frying: the high heat concentrates the flavour and caramelizes the juices. Serve them as a starter.

Sever the stems and strip off any tough strings and tiny leaves. Halve the stems lengthwise if they are thicker than your little finger. Depending on their size, quarter or halve the artichoke heads. Sprinkle the cut surfaces with a little lemon juice and plenty of salt.

Heat two-fingers' depth of oil in a small frying-pan (skillet) until it becomes lightly hazed with smoke – it should fry a cube of bread golden immediately.

Drop in the artichokes and stalks – only a few at a time so that the oil temperature does not drop too much. When the leaves are quite crisp and brown and the hearts and stalks feel soft when prodded with the point of a knife, remove the artichokes from the pan and drain well on kitchen paper.

Serve piled up on a pretty dish, with lemon quarters. *Manzanilla* – the dry, almost salty, white wine of Sanlúcar – tastes wonderful with the oily, sweet-yet-salty juices of the crisp artichokes.

Riñones al Jérez
Kidneys with sherry

1 veal kidney or 4 lamb's
   kidneys, skinned and
   de-veined
1 teaspoon wine vinegar
1oz/25g lard, or
   2 tablespoons olive oil
1 onion, skinned and
   finely chopped
1 teaspoon *pimentón*
Black pepper
1 glass dry sherry
1 tablespoon fresh
   breadcrumbs
1 garlic clove, skinned
   and finely chopped
1 tablespoon finely
   chopped parsley
1 bay leaf

Serves 2

Marinated kidneys is not an unusual complaint in the bars of Andalucía. This is the classic dish of Spain's most famous wine-growers. The local hair-of-the-dog hangover cure is a measure of oloroso *sherry, aromatic, dry and dark, diluted with tonic water.*

Slice the kidney finely, and scald it with hot water to which the vinegar has been added (to remove the faint taste of ammonia to which it is necessarily prone). Drain and dry.

Melt the lard or warm the oil in a small flameproof casserole. Toss in the chopped onion and let it fry gently until soft and golden. Add the kidney slices and turn them in the hot oil. Sprinkle in the *pimentón* and plenty of black pepper.

Pour in the sherry, turn up the heat, and allow it all to bubble up. Stir in the breadcrumbs, garlic, parsley and bay leaf. Turn down the heat and simmer gently for 10 minutes.

Accompany with chunks of good rough bread, a glass of the same dry sherry as in the sauce, and a salad of chopped cos lettuce mixed with olives and slivers of mild purple onion.

Bifteck salteado al Jérez

Grilled steak with wine

2 rump steaks
1 teaspoon olive oil
2 tablespoons roughly
   crushed peppercorns
1 teaspoon sherry vinegar
1 teaspoon Worcester
   sauce
1 small glass *oloroso*
   sherry
1oz/25g/¼ stick butter
Salt

Serves 2

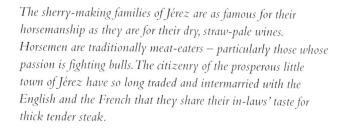

The sherry-making families of Jérez are as famous for their horsemanship as they are for their dry, straw-pale wines. Horsemen are traditionally meat-eaters – particularly those whose passion is fighting bulls. The citizenry of the prosperous little town of Jérez have so long traded and intermarried with the English and the French that they share their in-laws' taste for thick tender steak.

Rub the steaks with the oil and press both sides in the crushed peppercorns. Leave them for 30 minutes to absorb the flavour from the pepper.

Heat a griddle or heavy frying-pan (skillet). Slap on the steaks and sear them on each side for 2 minutes – turn down the heat and leave them longer if you like your steak well done.

Remove the steaks to a warm plate. Splash the vinegar, Worcester sauce and sherry into the hot pan, scrape in all the little caramelized bits, and let it all bubble up for a minute or two to evaporate the alcohol. Remove from the heat and whisk in the butter to thicken the sauce. Taste and add salt, then pour the sauce over the steaks.

Serve the steaks French-style with matchstick chips and buttered spinach dressed with grated nutmeg. Finish the meal with stuffed pancakes (*Crepas rellenas*, see page 94).

Manos de ternera
al horno con macarrones
Pot-roasted veal knuckles with macaroni

**4 veal knuckles or *osso
bucco* (shin of veal cut
right across the bone)**
2 tablespoons *pimentón*
**1 tablespoon crushed
peppercorns**
1 tablespoon salt
**1 tablespoon chopped
marjoram or oregano**
**4 tablespoons chopped
parsley**
2-3 bay leaves
**2 large onions, skinned
and chopped**
**6 garlic cloves, skinned
and sliced**
**2 glasses sherry or white
wine**
2 glasses water
**4oz/125g pork dripping
or olive oil**

To finish
**8oz/250g tube-shaped
macaroni**
Salt
1 tablespoon olive oil

Serves 4

*Made with young beef from the bull ranches of Jérez's hinterland,
this is a baker's dish, put to cook slowly as the oven cools after the
bread-making. The relationship between bread and wine is more
than just good friends: the yeast which leavens the dough is a
natural product of the wine-fermentation process, and an essential
to which the housewives of Jérez have had easy access since
Roman times. The Romans themselves much admired the white
bread of Andalucía. White-washed adobe ovens, built to the
Roman pattern, are still to be glimpsed tucked into a corner of
farmyards all over the province.*

Rub the meat with the spices, salt and herbs and arrange it in
a single layer in a roasting tin (pan) or shallow earthenware
dish. Sprinkle with the chopped onions and garlic. Pour in
the sherry and water. Dot with the dripping or trickle with
the olive oil.

Cover loosely with foil and put it to braise in the oven at
375°F, 160°C, Gas Mark 5 for 60-80 minutes, removing the
foil after the first 40 minutes, until the meat is falling off the
bone and deliciously brown, and the juices have cooked
down to a sticky sauce.

Cook the macaroni until soft in plenty of
boiling salted water. Drain it well, turn it in a
little olive oil, then tip into the meat dish
and coat with the juices. Serve all together,
piping hot.

Ensalada de tomates
Tomato Salad

2-3 beef tomatoes
2 fat garlic cloves,
    skinned and finely
    sliced
1 tablespoon chopped
    marjoram or flat-
    leaved parsley
3-4 tablespoons olive oil
Black pepper
Sugar

Serves 4

Spanish tomatoes are large, firm-fleshed, sweet and juicy. Dressed with olive oil, salt and slivers of the mild garlic of Andalucía, they refresh the palate and help the digestion after a heavy meat dish such as roast veal.

Slice the tomatoes finely and lay them on a flat dish. Sprinkle them with the sliced garlic and marjoram or parsley. Trickle the olive oil over the top and finish with a sprinkle of coarsely-milled black pepper and a little sugar.

Pavo en pepitoria
Turkey with nut sauce

6-8lb/3-4kg young
　turkey
6oz/175g lard or olive oil
1 thick slice bread, cubed
2 garlic cloves, skinned
Small bunch flat-leaved
　parsley
1 bay leaf
2oz/50g/1⅓ cup
　blanched almonds
1 teaspoon ground
　saffron or turmeric
　(known in Spanish
　markets as Indian
　saffron)
1 large onion, skinned
　and finely chopped
1 teaspoon ground cloves
1 teaspoon ground
　cinnamon
1 teaspoon ground white
　pepper
1 teaspoon ground
　allspice
Salt
Grated zest and juice of
　½ lemon

Serves 8

The turkey is a New World import, brought back to the ports of Andalucía from Mexico by the Jesuits. The monks, ever astute in the marketplace, kept a monopoly on the bird for a century or so, supplying it at a premium as the ideal feast food, sanctified by holy provenance, for high days and holidays. Fine feathers to swell monastery coffers, indeed, and still commemorated in the occasional reference to the bird as 'the Jesuit'.

Joint the turkey into about 24 pieces, using a hammer to tap the knife through the bones.

Heat the lard or oil in a roomy flameproof casserole. Toss in the bread cubes and garlic and fry them until golden. Remove and put them in a mortar or a blender. Drop the parsley sprigs and bay leaf into the hot oil and fry them quickly.

Add them, along with the almonds and saffron or turmeric, to the mixture in the mortar or blender.

Add the onion to the remaining oil and fry it until it softens a little. Push it to one side and add the turkey pieces. Turn them in the hot oil for a few minutes, until the skin takes a little colour. Add the ground cloves, cinnamon, pepper, all-spice and salt, lemon zest and juice, and splash in a glass of water. Let it bubble up, turn down the heat, cover, and cook gently for 30-40 minutes, until the meat is tender.

Meanwhile, work the mixture in the mortar or blender to make a thick paste. Stir the paste into the turkey juices when the meat is tender (you may need extra water). Bubble it all up, turn down the heat, and let it simmer gently for another 10 minutes or so to bring out and marry all the flavours.

Taste and adjust the seasoning. That's it: a dish as delicious as it is pretty. The fried paste – the *majado* – used to thicken the sauce is a medieval trick which seems to have survived in Andalucía long after it was replaced with flour-thickening elsewhere.

Berza de col
Stuffed cabbage

1lb/500g chickpeas,
   soaked for at least
   8 hours, or overnight
1-2 turnips, peeled and
   diced
2 thick slices fat bacon,
   diced
2oz/50g lard or olive oil
2 garlic cloves, skinned
   and finely chopped
1 teaspoon cumin seeds,
   crushed
1 tablespoon *pimentón*
1 handsome Savoy
   cabbage
8oz/250g minced pork
4oz/125g morcilla or
   other black pudding,
   skinned and mashed
1 tablespoon dried
   marjoram
1 egg, lightly forked
Salt and pepper

To finish (optional)
2oz/50g rice or soup
   vermicelli

Serves 6

This is a speciality of All Saints' Day and makes use of the winter vegetables and the autumn crop of chickpeas.

Drain and rinse the chickpeas and cover them with fresh water in a large saucepan. Bring to the boil and skim off the foam. Stir in the turnip, fat bacon and lard or olive oil and bring back to the boil. Turn the heat down a little, cover loosely with the lid and simmer for 1-1½ hours, adding boiling water when necessary. After 30-45 minutes, stir in the garlic with the cumin seeds and *pimentón*. When the chickpeas are tender, drain and reserve the stock.

Meanwhile, cut a deep cross in the stalk of the cabbage and scald it with boiling water so that you can splay the leaves more easily. Cut out the heart and chop it finely.

Mix the chickpeas with the chopped cabbage heart, minced pork, morcilla and dried marjoram, working in the egg to bind it. Season the mixture and use half to stuff between the leaves of the cabbage, pushing it well down towards the base. Form the remaining stuffing into a ball and drop it into the middle. Tie or skewer the cabbage firmly. Drop it into the large saucepan and pour the stock round it.

Bring the stock back to the boil, turn down the heat, cover, and simmer for 1 hour, until the cabbage is tender and the stuffing quite cooked.

Serve the stock first, as a soup, perhaps with a handful of rice or noodles poached in it, followed by the stuffed cabbage.

Torta imperial
Imperial layer-cake

For the base
5oz/150g/1⅓ cups
   ground almonds or
   hazelnuts
2 tablespoons cornflour
   (cornstarch)
10oz/300g/1¼ cups
   caster (superfine) sugar
6 egg whites

For the praline
4oz/125g/¾ cup
   almonds or hazelnuts
   (whole and unskinned)
8oz/250g/1 cup sugar

This delicious confection is Moorish in inspiration. After the Reconquest, the Andaluz middle-eastern sweet tooth was satisfied by the Catholic nuns, who made almond, egg and sugar confections for the Virgin's feast-days. This is my favourite.

First make the crisp nutty base. Mix together the ground almonds or hazelnuts, cornflour (cornstarch) and all but 6 tablespoons of the sugar. Whisk the egg whites until stiff, sprinkle in the remaining sugar and continue beating until the mixture forms a glossy meringue that holds peaks. Fold in the almond mixture.

Draw three 8 inch/20.5 cm circles on greaseproof paper and place them on three Swiss roll tins (jelly roll pans). Smooth the almond meringue inside the circles, and bake in the oven at 250°F, 120°C, Gas Mark 1 for 40-45 minutes, until crisp and dry. Transfer the rounds to a wire rack to cool.

Meanwhile, make the praline. Put the nuts and sugar in a small heavy-bottomed saucepan and heat gently, stirring until the sugar has dissolved. Continue to cook gently, until the sugar is caramelized to a deep golden brown and the nuts pop a little to show they are toasted (330°F, 165°C on a sugar thermometer). Spread the praline on an oiled tray or board and let it cool and harden. Crack it with a rolling pin or process briefly in a food processor – do not process for too long or it will turn into a paste.

For the caramel cream
3 tablespoons sugar
6 tablespoons water
4 egg yolks
8oz/250g/2 sticks
  unsalted butter,
  softened

Serves 8–10

Now make the caramel cream filling. In a small saucepan, dissolve the sugar in the water, then boil steadily until the syrup reaches the soft-ball stage: a clear, gluey syrup that registers 239°F, 115°C on the sugar thermometer. Beat the egg yolks and gradually pour in the hot syrup, beating constantly until the mixture cools to finger temperature. Cream the butter and beat it into the custard. Fold in half the praline.

To assemble the cake, spread about one quarter of the caramel cream on a meringue layer. Add the second layer, spread with more caramel cream and top with the remaining meringue layer. Spread the rest of the caramel cream over the top and sides. Finish with a dusting of the remaining praline. Put it in the fridge until firm, then cut into squares. (The meringue layers and cream filling can be frozen, then thawed and assembled later.)

Crepas rellenas
Stuffed pancakes

For the pancakes
2 eggs
4oz/125g/1 cup plain (all-purpose) flour
½ pint/300ml/1¼ cups milk
1oz/25g/2 tablespoons sugar
2oz/50g/½ stick butter

For the custard cream
3 egg yolks
½ pint/300ml/1¼ cups milk
3 tablespoons sugar
1oz/25g/¼ cup plain (all-purpose) flour
4oz/125g/1 stick unsalted butter
1 tablespoon brandy
Grated zest of 1 orange

Serves 4

This speciality of Jérez reflects the preferences of the town's chief trading partners. Here, French crepes are stuffed with English custard – the only gastronomic export with which England's cooks are universally credited.

To make the pancakes, put the eggs, flour, salt, milk and sugar in a blender or food processor and give it a good beating. Pour into a bowl and leave it to rest for 30 minutes.

Meanwhile, make the custard cream. Put the egg yolks, milk, sugar, flour and butter in the blender and beat it up. Pour the mixture into a small pan (if you prefer, use a bain-marie – a bowl balanced over a saucepan of boiling water) and bring it gently to just under the boil, beating all the while.

Cook gently for 5 minutes, then, when the custard is thick, take it off the heat and whisk in the brandy and the grated orange zest. Leave it on one side to cool.

To cook the pancakes, melt a small knob of butter in an omelette pan. Drop in a tablespoon of the pancake mixture and swirl it round the pan: it will set as soon as it touches the hot metal. Let the pancake cook until the edges curl. Flip it over and cook the other side. Remove and keep it warm under a cloth. Repeat until all the mixture is used up.

Roll each pancake round a little sausage of cooled custard and lay them in a gratin dish. Finish with a sprinkling of sugar and pop the dish under the grill (broiler) to caramelize the top.

Queso casero con pimentón
Farmhouse cheese with pimentón

**1lb/500g fresh curd
   cheese, or ricotta**
**1 yard/1 metre square of
   cheesecloth**
Salt
2-3 tablespoons olive oil
2oz/50g *pimentón*

Makes 1 cheese

Queso casero is home-made farm cheese. It keeps the distinctive print of the woven esparto grass basket in which it is put to drain. It is usually made with goat's milk turned with a curd from the stomach of the first kid of the spring (though vegetable rennet, particularly an infusion of thistles or artichoke hearts, is sometimes used instead). I used to get my cheeses from a neighbour down the valley who kept a small herd of goats to crop the herb-scented cistus scrub up and down the valley – and which would, on occasion, vary their diet among my flower pots. Sometimes my neighbour could be persuaded to sell me one of her special matured cheeses rubbed with olive oil and home-dried pimentón; or I would go up to the mountain village of Grazalema which has its own sheep's cheese – and very good it is too: salty and strong, but only made in spring and summer, when the sheep are in milk.

You can make your own curd cheese by squeezing a drop of lemon juice into some milk, and putting the curds to drip overnight in a cloth – tie the bag over the tap in the kitchen sink and save the whey for baking. 1 pint/600 ml of whole milk will yield only 3-4oz/75-100g, though, so it is more than a little expensive.

Put the cheese into the cheesecloth and pat it into a little round wheel. Sprinkle it with salt on both sides. Tie it up like a pocket handkerchief and put it on a cake rack to drain and dry out a little in a cool dry place. When it has firmed up, turn it over and let it dry on the other side. When it is quite firm, untie the cloth and rub the cheese all over with olive oil. Press the *pimentón* all over the outside. Put it back on its rack in the cool dry place and leave it for a week or so to form a crust and mature. Microbes never worried my goat-herding country-dwelling neighbour who would store her cheeses for months. But perhaps our modem cities have more lethal strains, so it is better to eat it relatively fresh.

A similar flavour can be enjoyed by mashing up the fresh cheese with *pimentón*, plenty of pepper, a little brandy, a dab of Tabasco and salt, and serving it as a potted cheese.

Córdoba

Córdoban home-cooking retains its strongly regional character. In the countryside, eggs feature strongly, as they do in all peasant farming communities, not only in the various *tortillas,* but also hard-boiled as garnishes for soups and pounded as a thickening for sauces. Breadcrumbs are used for Córdoba's native gazpacho, the *salmorejo;* for *migas,* a dish of fried savoury bread-crumbs which is effectively the winter gazpacho; and for thickening sauces. Moorish spicings prevail, but here lack the mint of Granada: imported nutmeg, cinnamon and cloves share shelf space with home-grown fennel seeds and saffron.

The New World's paprika, powdered or dried whole and torn into small pieces, adds additional sparkle. But you will not find many of these dishes in the restaurants of Córdoba – the province's rich culinary traditions have retreated in the face of mass tourism, and survive only in the kitchens of its hinterland.

Under the Moors, when its glorious mosque, the *mezquita,* was an important centre of pilgrimage, the city was renowned for the brilliance of its scholars, both Muslim and Jewish. The city stands on the northern bank of the Guadalquivir. To the north stretch the mineral-rich farmlands of the Sierra de Córdoba, to the south the olive groves and vineyards of the plains of Campiña.

Córdoba is a city of sudden pleasures: a glimpse of a shady patio supported on Roman pillars twined with jasmine and blue-hazed plumbago; the fountains and flowers of the old Jewish quarter, the Judería. Even the *mezquita* is buried like the kernel of an almond in the middle of the city's dwellings, its glorious forest of arches striped like football socks now ramparted by Christian stone walls. The city's artisans still specialize in silver-filigree, and the ancient tanning industry produces the oxtail stews that are to be found as a by-product in all leather-working towns.

The wines of Córdoba rival those of Jérez and are made in the same way. Moriles, Mantilla, Aguilar, Cabra, Lucena and Doña Mencía all produce recognizably different wines – best sampled with a plate of finely sliced *jamón serrano* (cured ham) and a dish of fennel-marinated green olives.

As for desserts, there is the usual bounty of Andalucían fruits, but particularly quinces and grenadines, with the little fruits of the *modroño, Arbutus unedo* or strawberry tree, as the favourite wild-gathered treat, and almonds, figs and raisins for the winter store cupboard.

Ajo sopeado

Gazpacho with garlic and salt cod

4oz/125g salt cod
   (bacalao), soaked and
   boned
4oz/125g pig's liver
6 tablespoons olive oil
4 garlic cloves,
   skinned and
   chopped
1lb/500g potatoes, peeled
   and diced
8oz/250g red peppers,
   hulled, de-seeded and
   chopped
1lb/500g tomatoes,
   scalded, skinned and
   chopped
4oz/125g fresh
   breadcrumbs
Salt and pepper

Serves 4

This dish, with its medieval flavours, is not for fainthearts. Traditionally served in the pan in which it has been cooked, the soup is scooped up with bread and a spoon. Choose salt cod (bacalao) *that is not too yellow, and check there is no thin line of blood down the spine which will tell you it has not been well salted. The middle cut is the best bit. Soak the salt fish for 48 hours, changing the water 3-4 times. A possible substitute is smoked haddock, which needs no soaking.*

Skin and pick the bones from the salt cod. Dice the liver. Heat the oil in a frying-pan (skillet) and put in the skinned garlic cloves. Fry them gently until they soften. Remove the garlic and put in the diced potatoes. Fry them gently until they soften, then take them out and put them to drain; sieve over a bowl to catch the drippings.

Reheat the oil drippings in the pan and put in the red peppers, liver and salt cod. Turn everything in the oil – add more if necessary – and cook gently for 10 minutes. Add the tomato pulp to the pan and bubble it up. Add the garlic and the potatoes, then pour in enough water to merge everything, and simmer gently for 10 minutes.

Stir in the breadcrumbs, season with salt, leave the pan on the side of the heat to thicken the sauce. Serve the *Ajo sopeado* as a hot dip with chunks of bread or crisp lettuce leaves to scoop it up.

Salmorejo

Córdoban gazpacho

2lb/1kg ripe tomatoes
10oz/300g stale bread,
  crumbed
2 garlic cloves, skinned
  and roughly chopped
1-2 tablespoons wine
  vinegar
¼ pint/150ml/⅔ cup
  olive oil
Salt and pepper
Sugar (optional)

To finish
2 hard-boiled eggs,
  peeled and sliced
4oz/125g *jamón serrano*
  cured ham or Parma
  ham, cut into small
  cubes

Serves 4

The Salmorejo of Córdoba is one of that venerable band of bread soups based on the leftovers from last week's baking, enlivened, post-Columbus, with New World tomatoes and peppers. Córdoba's gazpacho is quite solid – more of a hill-dweller's meal than the thin, iced soups of the coast. The Bar Los Arcos near the mezquita (mosque) does this fine version.

Either scald the tomatoes, and then skin and chop them, or (easier) halve and coarsely grate them, stopping before you get to the skin.

Put the tomatoes, breadcrumbs, garlic and vinegar in a blender or food processor and process the mixture to a puree. As it whizzes, gradually pour in the oil. Let the mixture sit for 1-2 hours in the refrigerator for the bread to swell. Add as much water as you need to make a thick soup which coats the back of a wooden spoon (if the tomatoes are watery, you will not need to add any). Taste, and add salt and pepper, and a little sugar if the tomatoes were not sun-ripened.

Divide the soup between 4 soup plates. Lay boiled egg on each serving and sprinkle with diced ham.

Migas canas

Fried bread and milk

1lb/500g stale bread
¼ pint/150ml/⅔ cup
   milk
Salt
6-8 tablespoons olive oil
1 garlic clove, skinned
   (optional, but usual)

To finish
½ pint/300ml/1¼ cups
   milk
1 teaspoon ground
   cinnamon (optional,
   but nice)

Serves 2-4

Migas are popular all over Spain, not just in Andalucía. They are served in the winter instead of summer's cold gazpachos, and are really a fried version of these rough peasant bread soups. As with all simple family dishes, there are as many variations as there are cooks. The basic recipe is soaked breadcrumbs, fried, rather as you might fry a hash. Rin-rán *is a local version which includes salt cod.* Carnerte, *another local recipe, mixes* migas *with fingers of bread soaked in beaten egg, folded and fried. Huelva has a version coloured with* pimentón *and mixed with fried* serrano *ham – in fact ham and pork scratchings are frequently included in recipes.*

This particular version served with milk, is the traditional rural breakfast in the cortijos *(farmsteads) of Córdoba's Province – and in the old days used to be eaten by the shepherds who drove their flocks great distances across Spain on the* Camino Real, *the annual transhumance route from winter to summer pasture.*

Cut the bread into cubes about the size of a chickpea, and sprinkle with lightly salted milk and water (only as much as the bread can absorb). Turn the cubes over a few times, and leave for 30 minutes to become spongy.

Heat the oil in a frying-pan (skillet) and add the garlic, if using. Fry it for a few minutes, and then remove and discard. Stir in the breadcrumbs and let them cook for about 10 minutes, stirring all the time, until they have separated and are well browned.

Sprinkle with cinnamon, if wished, and serve. Make a hole in the middle, as for porridge, and pour in some milk. Eat with a spoon, as you would a breakfast cereal.

Estofado de rabo de buey

Oxtail stew

4lb/2kg oxtails
8oz/250g butter beans
   or chickpeas, soaked
   for at least 8 hours or
   overnight
2 tablespoons olive oil
4oz/125g fatty *jamón
   serrano* cured ham, or
   streaky bacon, diced
1 large onion, skinned
   and chopped
2 garlic cloves, crushed
1 teaspoon salt
1 tablespoon *pimentón*,
   or 1 dried pepper,
   de-seeded and torn
1-2 small dried chillies,
   de-seeded and torn
1 short stick cinnamon
3-4 cloves
8-10 peppercorns, crushed
1 bay leaf
1lb/500g tomatoes,
   scalded, skinned
   and chopped
2 glasses *oloroso* sherry
   or red wine
Salt and pepper

Serves 6

All leather-working areas have recipes for Oxtail – a taste that dates back to the days when the skins for tanning came in with the tails still attached. No thrifty housewife could overlook such a valuable free bounty, and the tails went straight into the stew. Córdoba still has a vigorous leather-tooling industry, and continues to enjoy its oxtail stews.

Wipe and trim the excess fat off the oxtails and cut into joints. Drain the beans. Heat the oil in a flameproof earthenware casserole that will comfortably accommodate all the oxtail joints.

Turn the oxtail pieces in the hot oil. Remove them. Put in the ham or bacon, onion and garlic and fry gently until the vegetables soften. Return the oxtail to the casserole. Add the *pimentón*, chillies, cinnamon, cloves, peppercorns, bay leaf, butter beans or chickpeas, tomatoes and sherry or red wine.

Add enough water to submerge everything. Bring to the boil, lower the heat, cover tightly and leave to simmer either on top of the stove or in the oven at 300°F, 150°C, Gas Mark 2 for 3-4 hours, until the meat is practically falling off the bones. Check from time to time, and add more water if necessary. Taste and add salt and pepper.

Serve with a cos lettuce salad and chunks of bread. Finish off with some small sweet grapes or a ripe fig, and treat yourself to a glass of one of Rute's fine *aguardientes* (white brandies).

Cochifrito de conejo

Sweet-sour rabbit

1 wild rabbit, jointed (or 2lb/1kg rabbit joints)
1-2 tablespoons vinegar
1 teaspoon crushed peppercorns
¼ pint/150ml/⅔ cup olive oil
4 garlic cloves, skinned
Salt
1 bay leaf
1 tablespoon *pimentón*

Serves 3-4

A vinegar-spiked stew is a fine way to treat a rich, gluey meat such as kid or rabbit – and there are plentiful supplies of both in Córdoba's hinterland. This is the rural housewife's way with the marauders who fatten themselves on her carefully tended lettuces.

Pick over the rabbit, and chop the joints again if they are not bite-sized. Sprinkle the pieces with vinegar and rub them with the crushed peppercorns.

Heat the oil in a flameproof earthenware casserole or heavy saucepan. Put in the rabbit pieces and turn them in the hot oil until they turn a good colour.

Meanwhile, crush the garlic with a little salt. Stir in a glass of water and add the mixture to the rabbit. Bubble it up, lower the heat, tuck in the bay leaf and simmer gently, uncovered, for 30-40 minutes, until the rabbit is tender and all the juices have evaporated – or the meat, as the Andaluz say, is left in its own oils. Stir in the *pimentón* and take the pan off the heat before it burns.

Serve with thick-cut chips – they are nicest if you salt them *before* you fry.

Perdices en salmorejo

Partridges in tomato sauce

4 mature partridges
1 carrot, scraped and cut
    into chunks
1-2 sticks celery, chopped
½ onion, skinned
1 bay leaf
1 parsley sprig
4 peppercorns, crushed
Salt
1 glass dry Mantilla wine
    or sherry

For the sauce
8 tablespoons olive oil
1 red pepper, hulled,
    de-seeded and sliced
8 hard-boiled eggs,
    peeled
6 peppercorns, crushed
1 tablespoon *pimentón*
Salt and pepper

Serves 4

The red-legged partridge finds rich pickings in the vineyards of Mantilla; and those who tend the vines often swipe a brace for the pot at grape-harvesting time.

Clean and halve the partridges and put them in a saucepan with the carrot, celery, onion, herbs, peppercorns and salt.

Pour in the wine or sherry and enough water to submerge the partridges. Bring to the boil, turn down the heat, cover and simmer gently for about 1 hour, until the partridges are perfectly tender. Remove the birds and strain the stock.

To make the sauce, warm 2 tablespoons of the oil in a small frying-pan (skillet), put in the red pepper strips and let them fry gently until they soften. Tip the contents of the pan into a blender or a pestle and mortar with the yolks of the hard-boiled eggs, the crushed peppercorns and the *pimentón*. Process or pound to a pulp, trickling in the rest of the olive oil and adding a ladleful of the partridge stock.

Finely chop the egg whites and add them to the sauce. Dilute the sauce with as much of the partridge stock as you need to make about ¾ pint/450 ml/2 cups of sauce. Season.

Meanwhile, slip the partridges under a very hot grill (broiler) to blister the skin. Serve with the sauce poured around them.

Perrol de caceria

Rice-pot with game

2 partridges or pigeons, or 1 chicken
1 wild rabbit
¼ pint/150ml/⅔ cup olive oil
1 large onion, skinned and chopped
1 red pepper, hulled, de-seeded and chopped
1 tablespoon *pimentón*
8-10 saffron threads, soaked in a splash of hot water (or 1 teaspoon ground saffron)
1 large tomato, scalded, skinned and chopped
4-5 cloves
1 teaspoon grated nutmeg
1 bay leaf
1lb/500g Arborio (round-grain) rice
Salt and pepper

Serves 4-6

This juicy rice, a kind of soupy paella, is a party dish, made in quantity and served in the black iron casserole in which it is cooked. The recipe comes from the Venta Los Pela'os, at the foot of the bald-headed mountain from which the venta (roadside inn) takes its name. The mountain is crowned by the Sanctuary of the Virgin of the Sierra, patroness of the nearby town of Cabra. Her miraculous statue, garlanded with flowers and serenaded with rhyming couplets, is brought down from her mountain each September by her congregation. The procession crosses some rough terrain – the Lady has to be lowered down a series of canyons and precipices on ropes. The faithful follow the course of the underground stream which has its source from the Virgin's own spring. The waters make the land fertile, irrigating the olive plantations and feeding the wells of the town; and in this dry red earth, water is miracle enough.

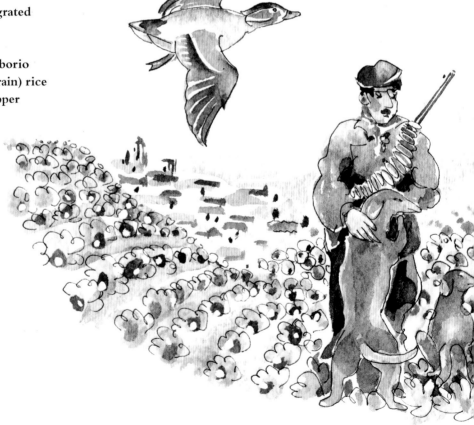

Wipe and joint the birds and the rabbit – the pieces should be bite-sized, as a *perrol* is eaten with a spoon, like a soup.
Heat the oil in a large deep pan. Throw in the onion and chopped pepper and the jointed meats, and fry until the vegetables soften and the meat seals and browns.

Sprinkle in the *pimentón* and add the saffron and its soaking liquid. Then add the tomato, cloves and nutmeg and let everything bubble up.

Pour in enough boiling water to submerge the meats completely (about 3 pints/2 litres/7½ cups). Tuck in the bay leaf, season with salt and pepper, and bring everything to the boil.

Turn down the heat, cover and leave to simmer for 1 hour, until the meats are perfectly tender.

Stir in the rice with a wooden spoon. The rice should be submerged to a depth of two fingers – add more boiling water if you need to. Bring all back to the boil, stirring until it gives one big belch, then turn down the heat and let the pot simmer for 20 minutes. The rice should be soupy, the texture of juicy rice pudding. Check the seasoning.

Take the pot off the heat and leave it on the side of the stove for 5 minutes. Serve the *perrol* in deep soup plates, with a fork and spoon and a big white napkin each.

Tortilla de patatas

Potato omelette

8 tablespoons olive oil
6 medium-sized potatoes,
  peeled and diced,
  sliced or cut into chips
½ large Spanish onion
  (or 1 ordinary one),
  skinned and chopped
6 large eggs
Salt

Serves 4

This is the proper food for any romería *(pilgrimage), including that to the sanctuary of Nuestra Señora de Cabra. Our Lady retains many characteristics of her predecessor, the hunter-goddess Artemis-Diana, so the young people of the town go up the mountain the evening before and spend a night out under the stars. As for the* tortilla, *some include parsley, some replace the onion with garlic, or leave both out altogether.*

Heat the oil in a frying-pan (skillet). Gently fry the potato and the onion in the oil, but do not let them take any colour. Transfer the potato and onion to a bowl.

Fork the eggs lightly with a little salt and add them to the potatoes. Pour most of the oil out of the pan, reheat it and tip in the egg mixture. Push the potatoes down into the egg. Fry gently on a low heat, until the eggs start to set. As it cooks, neaten the sides with a metal spatula to build up a deep straight edge to the *tortilla*. When it looks firm, slide it out onto a plate, then invert it back into the pan to cook the other side. You might need a little more oil.

Serve hot, or leave to cool and cut into squares for a picnic.

Caldillo de pollo
Farmhouse chicken with egg sauce

1 chicken, jointed into
   small pieces, and
   including the liver,
   neck and heart
1-2 tablespoons lard or
   olive oil
1 thick slice Spanish
   onion, chopped
1 garlic clove, skinned
   and chopped
Salt and pepper

For the sauce
1 hard-boiled egg
6-8 saffron threads,
   soaked in a splash
   of hot water (or 1
   teaspoon ground
   saffron)
1 garlic clove, skinned
   and roughly chopped
1 tablespoon vinegar
1 glass water
4-6 tablespoons olive oil

Serves 4

This is another of those peculiarly Córdoban dishes finished with a sauce thickened with pounded cooked egg yolk. The technique produces an emulsion, rather like a mayonnaise, so the sauce should not be hot, or it will separate. This caldillo, 'little soup', can be made with wild game (rabbit, partridge or pigeon) instead of the barnyard fowl.

Put the chicken joints in a roasting tin (pan), dot with lard or trickle with olive oil, sprinkle with the chopped onion and garlic, season with salt and pepper, and roast in the oven at 375°F, 190°C, Gas Mark 5 for 45-50 minutes, basting occasionally, until well browned and tender. (Andaluz cooks cook their chickens until the meat is falling off the bone.)

Meanwhile, make the sauce. Peel the egg, halve it and take out the yolk. Put the egg yolk, saffron, garlic, vinegar and water in a blender or food processor and combine the mixture thoroughly. Trickle in the oil as for a mayonnaise. Chop the egg white and stir it into the sauce.

Arrange the chicken on a pretty serving dish, and dress it with the sauce.

Serve warm but not hot, or the sauce will separate.

Migas de matanza
Pig-killing breadcrumbs

1lb/500g pig's liver

1 pig's kidney, cored and
    put to soak in vinegar
    and water

8oz/250g pork belly,
    cut into small cubes

4oz/125g kidney fat,
    cut into small cubes

¼ pint/150ml/⅔ cup
    olive oil

1lb/500g stale bread,
    cut into cubes the size
    of chickpeas

1 teaspoon *pimentón*

½ teaspoon crushed
    oregano

½ teaspoon fennel seeds

¼ teaspoon ground
    cloves

½ teaspoon ground
    cinnamon

Salt and pepper

Serves 4

Those who still keep their own pigs make their own blood pudding – morcilla, spiced with cloves, fennel and coriander seeds, oregano, pimentón and garlic – and pepper-spiced chorizo sausage. The hams are salt-cured in the dry mountain air. The meal prepared for those involved in the matanza (pig-killing ceremony) is this dish of migas (fried breadcrumbs), prepared with the more perishable parts of the animal.

Cube the liver and season it. Drain and dry the kidney, cube it and season it. Put these meats aside for the moment.

Heat the oil in a heavy frying-pan (skillet), and gently fry the cubes of pork belly and kidney fat for about 20 minutes, until they are crisp and brown, and have yielded up their fat.

Remove the pork cracklings and keep warm. Add the liver and kidney cubes to the pan. Let the meat fry gently for 15-20 minutes, until it is well cooked and tender and the oil is clear again. Take out the meat and keep it warm.

Off the heat, stir the spices and salt and pepper into the fat that remains in the pan, and pour in a wineglass of water. Return the pan to the heat and bubble it all up. Stir in the diced bread gradually until the liquid in the pan is all taken up. Let it cook gently for 15 minutes, stirring continually, until the breadcrumbs are separate and well browned. Take the pan off the heat, make a well in the middle of the *migas* and pile in the reserved cracklings and meats.

Set the pan in the middle of the table: *Migas de matanza* are traditionally eaten straight out of the pan with a spoon – each person tackling the section directly in front of him or her.

Chanfaina

Chicken stew with pork

1 boiling chicken, jointed
1lb/500g fillet of pork,
    neatly tied
1 glass dry sherry or
    white wine
1 large tomato, scalded,
    skinned and chopped
1 dried red pepper,
    de-seeded and torn,
    or ½ fresh red pepper,
    hulled, de-seeded and
    chopped
1 large onion, skinned
    and chopped
3 tablespoons olive oil
Salt and pepper
8oz/250g pig's liver,
    in one piece
8oz/250g morcilla or
    other black pudding,
    sliced
2 tablespoons
    breadcrumbs
2oz/50g/⅓ cup toasted
    almonds
1 teaspoon nutmeg
2-3 parsley sprigs

Serves 6-8

This is not a dish to be done by halves. You need an appreciative audience of at least six people with robust appetites. It's sometimes made with a small turkey rather than a chicken. These bronze-feathered barnyard birds of Andalucía, descended from stock brought back by the Jesuits from the New World, are muscular creatures, used to foraging for themselves, and no bigger than a large chicken.

Put the chicken portions and pork fillet into a saucepan which will just accommodate it, with the sherry or wine, tomato, red pepper, onion, oil, salt and pepper and enough water to submerge everything.

Bring it all to the boil and then turn down the heat, cover loosely and simmer for 20 minutes. Add the liver (still in one piece) and the morcilla. Bring back to the boil, turn down to simmer and cook for another 20-30 minutes.

Take out the liver – if it is not yet tender, leave it to simmer until it is. Roughly chop the liver and put it in a blender or food processor with the breadcrumbs, almonds, nutmeg, plenty of freshly milled black pepper and a ladleful of the cooking liquor from the meat. Process to a thick sauce.

When the chicken and the pork are tender, stir the liver sauce into the broth with the parsley. Reheat and simmer gently for another 10 minutes. Taste and add salt and pepper.

Serve with chunks of bread, plain rice or mashed potato.

Lomo en adobo

Spiced pork fillet

1lb/500g pork fillet
2 tablespoons *pimentón*
1 teaspoon chopped
  oregano
1 garlic clove, crushed
1 teaspoon salt
1 tablespoon olive oil

Serves 4

The best part of the pig, the long back fillet, is either spiced and dried whole, or gently stewed and potted in pimentón-*flavoured lard; or it can be marinated overnight and roasted in a closed pot.*

Pat the pork fillet dry. Mix the *pimentón*, oregano, garlic and salt with the oil. Rub the pork fillet thoroughly with this mixture. Wrap it in foil, and leave it in the refrigerator overnight, preferably longer. The meat can be kept in its marinade for a week – improving daily.

When you are ready to cook the fillet, make sure it is sealed in its foil and bake it in the oven at 350°F, 180°C, Gas Mark 4 for 45-60 minutes, depending on the thickness of the fillet, then at 325°F, 170°C, Gas Mark 3 for 10 minutes. Remove from the oven and let the meat cool in its foil.

Slice the fillet on the diagonal, and serve it with a big plate of crisp chips, bread and a tomato and sweet onion salad.

Tortilla a la payesa
Peasant omelette

All Europe has its own version of bacon and eggs – the two ingredients to which rural housewives had easy access. At its simplest, this omelette is just eggs, potatoes and bacon, but this version has spring vegetables as well. Other vegetables, including wild greens, might go in at different times of year, and, in winter, a few cooked chickpeas or haricots as well. It's sometimes served up under the name of Granada's Tortilla Sacromonte *(see page 21).*

Fork the eggs lightly together with salt and pepper – the white and the yolk should not be perfectly mixed.

Heat 3 tablespoons of oil in an omelette pan. Put in the potato cubes or slices, and cook them gently until tender – they should take a little colour. Remove them and put them to drain in a sieve over a bowl to catch the drippings.

5 eggs
Salt and pepper
4-5 tablespoons olive oil
1 large potato, peeled and
**   diced or finely sliced**
2oz/50g *jamón serrano*
**   cured ham,**
**   or gammon, diced**
1 garlic clove, skinned
**   and chopped**
1 slice onion, chopped
1 small tomato, chopped
4 tablespoons shelled,
**   cooked peas**
**   (fresh or frozen)**
4oz/125g green beans,
**   topped-and-tailed,**
**   chopped into short**
**   lengths and cooked**

Serves 4

Reheat the oil. Add the ham or gammon, garlic and onion. Fry gently until everything has softened and taken some colour. Add the tomato and bubble up to evaporate off the excess liquid.

Mix the egg with the potatoes, peas and beans and the contents of the omelette pan. Wipe the pan, put in the rest of the oil, and heat it. Tip in the egg mixture and cook the omelette as you would a thick pancake.

Neaten and build up the sides with a spatula as the tortilla cooks, turning once – be brave and flip it over on to a plate, and then slide it back into the pan. You may need to add a little extra oil.

Serve warm or cool: the perfect meal-in-a-piece.

Olla cordobense

Córdoban chickpea stew

The countryman's dish, this is the hot-pot of the day-labourer, a simple, nourishing, one-pot soup-stew eaten with bread and a spoon. Use seasonal greens – in winter, cabbage, but at other times of year, spinach, chard, artichokes or wild greens. There are no rules with a dish like this – include any herbs that take your fancy, plus celery, onion, turnip (with tops), whatever.

1lb/500g chickpeas, soaked for at least 8 hours or overnight

8oz/250g fat bacon in a piece, or a bacon hock

4oz/125g trimmings and fat from *jamón serrano* cured ham

3-4 garlic cloves in a bunch

5-6 saffron threads

1 dried red pepper, de-seeded and torn, or ½ fresh red pepper, hulled, de-seeded and chopped

1 carrot, scraped and cut into chunks

6 peppercorns, crushed

1 bay leaf

3 tablespoons olive oil

1 large potato, peeled and cut into chunks

1lb/500g green cabbage

Salt

Serves 4–6

Drain the chickpeas and put them in a large pot with the bacon and ham trimmings. Singe the garlic in a flame, and roast the saffron in a metal spoon over a flame, to release the flavour. Add these to the pot and pour in enough cold water to submerge everything to a depth of two fingers.

Stir in the pepper, carrot, peppercorns, bay leaf and olive oil. Bring to the boil, cover loosely and cook for 2-3 hours, until the chickpeas are tender. Do not let the pot come off a slow boil – the chickpeas do not soften if the pot stops boiling. Add boiling water when it is needed.

Add the potato and bring everything back to boil. Cook for 10 minutes, then add the cabbage. Season with salt. Everything should be ready in another 10 minutes. Take out the bacon and dice it – if you have used a bacon hock, take the meat off the bone and return the meat to the stew. Serve with bread and a spoon.

Horchata

Nut milk

8oz/250g/2¼ cups
  ground almonds
2 pints/1.2 litres/5 cups
  water
2 tablespoons sugar
  (more or less, as you
  please)
1 short cinnamon stick

*Makes 2 pints / 1.2 litres /
  5 cups*

*This refrigerating infusion of ground-up nuts is another legacy of
Moorish rule. These days, you can buy it in concentrated form, or
fresh, in cartons, from the dairy section of the supermarket. Many
towns have an* horchatería *which does double duty as a milk bar.
The commercial variety is made with tigernuts* (chufas).

Stir the ground almonds into the water and leave to infuse
overnight. Next day, strain the liquid into a saucepan (use the
nut residue to make *Ajo blanco* – see page 49), stir in the sugar
and bring the liquid to boiling point, stirring as the sugar
dissolves. Add the cinnamon stick. Leave it on the side of the
stove to cool.

Chill in the refrigerator, and remove the cinnamon stick just
before serving. It makes a delicious refreshing summer
drink – just right for the hot plains in summer, the 'frying-
pan' of Spain.

Fideos dulces

Honeyed noodles

6oz/180g/1½ cups self-
 raising flour
½ teaspoon salt
3 eggs
1 tablespoon oil
Oil for frying
1lb/500g/1⅓ cups honey

Serves 4

Doughnuts and noodle-fritters are festival foods all over Europe – particularly for carnival and the celebrations that immediately precede the Lent fast. These honey-soaked egg noodles come in many shapes and sizes, so you can make up your own: the dough can be cut into circles, stars, whatever you please.

Sieve the flour with the salt into a bowl. Make a dip in the middle and work in the eggs and the oil with your hand, drawing in enough flour to give you a firm, pliable dough. Let the dough rest for 20 minutes.

Cut the dough in half. On a well-floured board, roll it out so thin that you can see the wood-grain through it. Cut the dough into fine strips, lightly flour them and drop them in heaps on to the board.

Put a deep panful of oil on to heat – when it is lightly hazed with smoke, drop in a cube of bread: if it fries golden immediately, the oil is the right temperature. Add the noodles, a handful at a time, and fry them until golden. Remove and drain on kitchen paper. Meanwhile, melt the honey with a little water in a small pan. Trickle the warm honey-syrup over the noodles, and serve.

Dulce de membrillo

Quince paste

*Quince paste is the most famous Córdoban sweetmeat –
particularly that made in Puente Genil, which
comes in blue tins and brings back memories of
childhood Christmases to every exiled
Córdoban. Quince paste was the original
'marmalade', and to a medieval beauty a gift
of quince was a declaration of love. A ripe
quince has a deliciously flowery scent.*

4lb/2kg ripe quinces
**About 3 pints/1.75
    litres/7½ cups water**
**About 4lb/2kg/8 cups
    preserving sugar**

Makes about 6lb/3kg paste

Wipe and roughly chop the quinces and put them
in the water immediately, to prevent blackening. Bring to the
boil, turn down to a simmer, and cook until the quince flesh
is soft (do not boil them too long or they turn red and the
colour of the paste will be too dark).

Push the flesh, juice and all, through a sieve with the back of
a spoon. Weigh the pulp and stir in 1lb/500g/2 cups of sugar
for each 1lb/500g of fruit.

Bring very gently to the boil in a heavy pan, stirring until all
the sugar has dissolved. Either spread the paste on the bottom
of a lightly oiled baking tin (pan) and leave in a very low
oven to dry out overnight, or simmer for 30-35 minutes
(until the pulp pulls away from the sides of the pan), and then
spread it on the bottom of a baking tin to set.

When it is cool, cut the paste into squares, wrap it neatly in
greaseproof paper, and store in a dry cupboard. Delicious
with cheese, the paste hardens and darkens as it matures.

Sevilla

The NATURAL CAPITAL OF Andalucía, Sevilla contains all that is best and worst of the region. The Golden City has always been home to princes and beggars, priests and courtesans, poets and thieves. The centre of the city, the Sierpes, is given over to luxury shops and busy merchants. The pavement cafés and alleyway bars are crowded day and night; Sevilla is the birthplace of the tapa bar, where the citizenry can take a sip of sherry, Andalucía's house-wine, and take the edge off their appetite with a tiny portion of what will probably be on the menu for dinner later – much later. In the narrow streets of the old Barrio Santa Cruz, gypsies from Triana across the river tell the fortunes of the scholars hurrying to the Archive of the Indies.

The sixteenth century was the city's Golden Age. Notorious as the Babylon of Spain, Sevilla was also, effectively, the capital of the New World. Her merchant princes, coffers bulging with raided gold, employed the skilled craftsmen, those same who had learned their trade from Moorish masters, to build magnificent palaces to accommodate their spoils. Her port was hectic with traffic for the New Indias, her warehouses crammed with exotic treasures. The mighty River Guadalquivir, life-blood of Andalucía, had not yet silted up, forcing Sevilla's wealth and custom to Cádiz.

But the gold of the Americas was not its most valuable treasure: the vegetables of the New World revolutionized the diet of all Europe and much of Africa: tomatoes and peppers, pumpkins and marrows, maize and haricot beans, all were ideally suited to the fertile earth of Andalucía. The potato was at first treated with much suspicion, accused of harbouring leprosy and causing unknown plagues. Nevertheless, noble ladies liked its pretty blossoms, and planted the tubers in the patios of their palaces: it was from the flowerpots of Sevilla that the tuber colonized the Old World.

Centuries of trading has ensured Sevilla a quietly prosperous bourgeoisie and a well-heeled bureaucracy. This is a city of wealthy burghers whose wives keep a well-stocked larder: the towns-folk like to eat richly, leisurely and in good company.

Sevilla is still a glamorous city, its grace derived in part from ethereal towers rising from seething, shadowy alleyways, in part from the fertile plain which nourishes it. The red-earthed countryside which surrounds the city has long been planted with shady groves of olives, vines, oranges, lemons and almonds. Here, visible and to hand, are the raw materials essential to a fine culinary tradition.

White-walled farmhouses powder the rolling fields: many peasants still keep their own pigs, salt their own hams and make their own varieties of cheese. Morón de la Frontera makes a famous cheese, mostly from cow's milk, which can be eaten fresh or aged in olive oil – the older the cheese, the harder and spicier it becomes. Here, too, is fruit in abundance. Grapes of course, and peaches and apricots, custard apples and quinces, pomegranates and persimmons – a garden of paradise; and the whole province makes beautiful jams and jellies from its soft summer fruits. The rural households of Sevilla's province eat very well indeed.

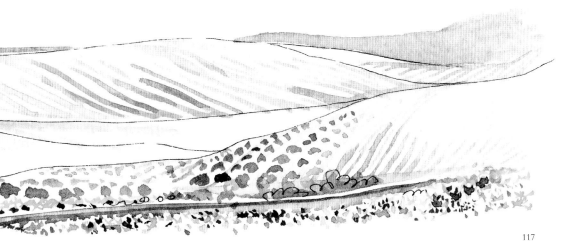

Aceitunas aliñadas áromaticas

Aromatic pickled olives

1lb/500g whole, unstoned
(unpitted) green olives
4 garlic cloves, left in
their skins and singed
in a flame
1 bitter orange, or lemon
1-2 thyme sprigs
1 tablespoon coriander
seeds
1 stick dried fennel,
broken into short
lengths
1 small glass sherry
or wine vinegar

Makes 1lb/500g olives

The pickled olives of Sevilla are famous – the natural tapa or 'lid' for a glass of sherry, the house-wine of Andalucía. I used to pickle my own fresh olives every year. The fruit had to be cracked before soaking – a chore my four children performed with gusto and a hammer. The olive stones (pits) shot into every corner, and the black juice freckled everything and everyone. Here is my own marinade – in default of fresh olives, it gives a kick to commercially prepared ones.

Drain the olives and bash them lightly with a rolling pin. Bash each singed garlic clove once. Cut a slice from the middle of the orange or lemon and roughly dice the rest.

Pack everything into a screw-top jar, and top up with enough water to cover. Top with the orange or lemon slice to keep the olives submerged. You should not need extra salt as shop-bought preserved olives have plenty of their own.

Screw on the lid tightly and keep in the refrigerator for at least a week. Bring the olives up to room temperature before serving them.

Ensalada sevillana

Sevillan salad

1 *escarola* (frizzy endive)
1 red pepper
½ cucumber
2-3 slices mild onion
1 tablespoon capers
4 tablespoons green
   olives stuffed with
   anchovies
A few tarragon leaves

For the dressing
1 hard-boiled egg
1 garlic clove
8 tablespoons olive oil
2 tablespoons sherry
   vinegar

Serves 4

The particularly Sevillan ingredient in this salad is the tarragon, a herb not much used in Spain. And in Sevilla you can get small red peppers – guindillas – to decorate the salad. As with all such composite first-course salads, it is highly variable and may include whatever the cook feels appropriate in the way of artichoke hearts, cooked beans, canned tuna, tomatoes and cucumbers. I like my salads simple: this version is quite complicated enough as it is.

Rinse and tear the *escarola*. Hull, de-seed and slice the pepper into fine rings. Slice the cucumber.

Arrange all the salad ingredients, layering them in roughly the order they are listed, in a shallow dish.

To make the dressing, peel the hard-boiled egg, remove the yolk, and mash it with the garlic, oil and vinegar. Dress the salad with this piquant cream. Finish with a sprinkling of finely chopped egg white and sea salt.

Almejas a la marinera
Clams in tomato sauce

2lb/1kg fresh clams (or any small bi-valve, such as mussels) in the shell
2 tablespoons olive oil
1 onion, skinned and chopped
2 garlic cloves, skinned and chopped
8oz/250g tomatoes, scalded, skinned and chopped
1 teaspoon *pimentón*
1 generous glass dry sherry or white wine
2 tablespoons chopped parsley

Serves 4

Sevilla enjoys its shellfish – mariscos – and many of its bars and restaurants are devoted to them, selling them by weight and preparing them on the instant, to order. Triana, the old gypsy quarter, is the place to seek out the best shellfish. To see the debris of a Saturday evening, one might think the city itself is built on the shells of a million molluscs.

Rinse the shellfish, checking over and discarding any that are broken or gape open.

Put the oil to heat in a wide shallow pan, preferably one with a lid. Toss in the onion and garlic and let them fry gently until they soften and take a little colour. Add the tomatoes and *pimentón*, turn up the heat, and let it all cook down for a few minutes to concentrate the flavours. Pour in the sherry or wine, let it come to the boil again, and add the parsley and then the shellfish.

Turn up the heat, and cover with a lid, shaking the pan to redistribute the shells so that all have a chance to cook thoroughly. If you have no lid, keep moving the clams around the pan with a spatula.

It will take 3-4 minutes for all the shells to open. Take them off the heat immediately. It doesn't matter if you keep them on one side for a few minutes – they'll be easier to eat when they cool down a little – but don't reheat them or they turn to India rubber.

Everyone sucks the shells – so you will need bread for wiping fingers and mopping up the sauce.

Espárragos a la parilla
Grilled asparagus

1½lb/750g best medium-
thick green asparagus
Olive oil
Sea salt

For the sauce
6-8 parsley sprigs
1-2 tarragon sprigs
2-3 spring onions
(scallions), green and
white parts, washed
and chopped
1 garlic clove, skinned
1 teaspoon French
mustard
½ teaspoon freshly milled
black pepper
6-8 tablespoons olive oil
1 tablespoon wine
vinegar

Serves 4 as a starter

The sandy gardens west of Sevilla produce fine asparagus. In Spain, asparagus is only ever blanched if it is to be conserved – when it is considered a great luxury, even when fresh asparagus is available. Nevertheless, the Spaniard likes his fresh native asparagus green and tender. This is how I had it prepared in one of the restaurants in the Barrio Santa Cruz. The parilla, a built-in grill (broiler) plate, is the favourite implement of the Andaluz short-order cook, whether housewife or restaurant chef. It's perfect for fillets of fish or meat – and a stroke of genius to think of applying its sizzling dry heat to fresh green asparagus. You will never want to cook it any other way: the flavour is incomparable.

Wash and trim the asparagus, discarding the woody bits and peeling off any hard skin. Brush each spear all over with olive oil, paying particular attention to the tips. Sprinkle the spears with the rough sea salt crystals.

Put all the sauce ingredients in a blender or food processor and puree them to a thick green sauce.

Grill the asparagus until it steams and blisters black. Turn it over and grill the other side. Serve hot, with the green sauce for dipping.

Pez espada a la plancha
Grilled swordfish with oregano

1lb/500g swordfish steaks
2 tablespoons olive oil
Juice of 1 lemon
2 garlic cloves, skinned
   and chopped
1 tablespoon chopped
   oregano or marjoram
1 tablespoon chopped
   parsley
Salt and pepper

Serves 6 as a starter,
   4 as a main course

Swordfish is much prized in Andalucía. It's considered as good as meat – the sea's equivalent of the fillet steak. This is a rich man's fish, proper food for the grandees of the Golden City, whose gates bear the legend 'Hercules built me, Caesar fortified me, the King Saint delivered me'.

Rub the swordfish steaks with the oil and lemon juice, and sprinkle with the garlic, herbs, salt and plenty of freshly milled black pepper. Let the fish marinate for 1-2 hours.

Heat a griddle or grill (broiler) to maximum heat. Grill (broil) the steaks fiercely and briefly – marinading tenderizes them and makes them cook more easily.

Serve with quartered lemons and bread as a starter, or with mashed potato or rice as a main course.

Ternera mechada a la sevillana
Braised larded veal

1lb/1kg boned veal
   shoulder, rolled
   and tied
12 stoned (pitted) green
   olives stuffed with
   pimiento
12 toasted almonds
1oz/25g lard
1 onion, skinned and
   chopped
2 garlic cloves, skinned
   and chopped
1 teaspoon *pimentón*
1 glass *Mantilla,* dry
   sherry or white wine
½ pint/300ml/1¼ cups
   water or stock
1 short cinnamon stick

To finish
1 glass sherry
   or white wine
2 tablespoons tomato
   purée

Serves 6

This sophisticated pot-roast betrays the cosmopolitan influences of the city-port. It's unusually pretty – as a rule, the Andaluz kitchen concerns itself more with flavour than presentation. I am told the proper broth is made with the dry pale wine of Mantilla, which has a fair, though vigorously disputed, claim to antedate Jérez' more celebrated product.

Using a sharp knife, make thin incisions deep into the centre of the meat (lengthwise cuts are best) and push in the olives and almonds.

Melt the lard in a flameproof casserole that will just about accommodate the joint, and toss in the onion and garlic. Let it fry for a moment or two, and then put in the meat. Turn it in the hot fat until it takes a little colour. Add the *pimentón,* the *Mantilla,* sherry or white wine and the water or stock, and let it all bubble up.

Tuck in the cinnamon stick, cover tightly and leave it to braise either on a gentle heat on top of the stove or in the oven at 350°F, 180°C, Gas Mark 4 for an hour or so, until the meat is quite tender and the juices have evaporated right down to an oily slick.

Let the meat settle for 15 minutes or so, and then carve it into thick slices. Arrange these overlapping on a dish and keep warm.

To finish, pour the sherry or white wine into the casserole and scrape in all the sticky bits. Let it bubble up to evaporate the alcohol. Stir in the tomato puree, taste, and add salt and pepper if necessary. Pour this sauce over the meat just before serving it, French-style, with smooth, creamy mashed potato.

Dorada a la sal

Salt-baked sea bream

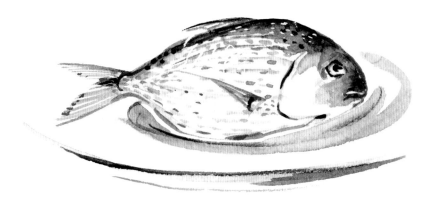

2–4lb/1–2kg whole
   sea bream, or other
   large, firm-fleshed
   fish, neither gutted nor
   scaled
1 egg white
3 tablespoons water
2lb/1kg (at least) sea salt

Serves 4–6

*This is the speciality of Sevilla's best fish restaurant, the epony-
mous 'La Dorada'. Once sacred to sea-born Venus, the
golden-headed bream is a beautiful broad-flanked silver fish with
golden markings. This excellent method of cooking it conserves the
juices without in any way over-salting the flesh. The quantity of
salt is rather daunting unless you have your own salt flats just
down the road – in an emergency I use dishwasher salt.*

Choose a long baking dish which will comfortably take the
whole fish. Wipe the fish but do not scale or gut it. Pour
enough salt in the dish to make a layer 1 inch/2.5 cm thick.

Mix the egg white with the water and sprinkle half the liquid
over the salt. Lay the fish on the salt bed and pour enough salt
around and over it to cover it completely. Sprinkle with the
remaining egg white and water. Bake it in the oven at 375°F,
190°C, Gas Mark 5 for about 1 hour, the temperature adjusted
up or down depending on the size of the fish.

Place the fish, still encased in its snowy armour, in the middle
of the table. Crack open the salt crust with a hammer. A little
theatricality is quite proper to Venus's favourite. The skin will
come off with the salt, revealing perfectly cooked, succulent
flesh without a trace of saltiness.

Serve the fish with quartered lemons and a jug of the thickest,
greenest virgin olive oil you can find.

Gambas en gabardina
Prawns in raincoats

12-18 large cooked
  prawns (shrimp)
1 pint/600ml/2½ cups
  water
1 small glass dry sherry
Bouquet garni (bay leaf,
  thyme, parsley, tied
  together)
½ onion, skinned
3 tablespoons olive oil,
  or 4oz/125g/1 stick
  butter
3oz/75g/¾ cup plain
  (all-purpose) flour
Salt and pepper

For the coating
3 tablespoons seasoned
  flour
1 egg beaten with
  2 tablespoons milk
4-5 tablespoons toasted
  breadcrumbs
Oil for frying

Serves 4 as a starter

My favourite public palace is the hotel Alfonso XIII in the heart of Sevilla. Although built at the beginning of this century, it has marvellous Moorish azulejos – another legacy of the Almohad caliphs, who taught the craftsmen of Triana the secret of these rainbow-glazed tiles. It was among the orange trees on the intricately carved patio of the hotel that I first had these crisp-jacketed prawns, the best of Andalucía's tribe of croquettes, as the tapa to accompany a mimosa – a long drink of champagne with freshly squeezed orange juice.

Peel the prawns (shrimp), but leave the tails on. Put the peelings, heads and all, in a saucepan with the water, sherry, *bouquet garni* and onion. Bring to the boil, turn down the heat and simmer for 20-30 minutes, until you have ¾ pint/450 ml/2 cups well-flavoured stock. Sieve the stock, discarding the solids.

Heat the oil or butter in a saucepan. Stir in the plain (all-purpose) flour and let it froth up for a moment. Gradually beat in the prawn stock with a wooden spoon. Cook it over a gentle heat until you have a very thick, soft sauce – the more skilful you become, the thinner you can make the sauce, and the more delicate the croquettes will be. Taste and season with salt and pepper.

Dip the prawns in the sauce to coat them all over, leaving the little pink tails exposed. Leave them for 1-2 hours to become cool and firm.

To make the coating, spread the seasoned flour on one plate, the egg and milk mixture on a second and the breadcrumbs on a third. First, dust each sauce-coated prawn with flour, then dip it in the egg mixture, and finally press it firmly into the breadcrumbs.

Heat two-fingers' depth of oil in a frying-pan (skillet). When it is lightly hazed with smoke and a cube of bread will fry golden in it immediately, slip in the prawns a few at a time – not too many at once or the oil temperature will drop. Fry them until crisp and golden brown. Serve the prawns hot from the pan, with quartered lemons and garlic mayonnaise.

Menudo gitano
Gypsy tripe

1lb/500g prepared tripe

8oz/250g chickpeas,
soaked for at least
8 hours or overnight

1 calf's foot, blanched
and split, or 1 pig's
trotter, split

A short length of ham
bone, or a small piece
of bacon

1 onion, skinned and
chopped

2 garlic cloves, left in
their skins and singed
in a flame

1 parsley sprig and
1 mint sprig

1 bay leaf

½ teaspoon peppercorns,
crushed

Salt

For the sofrito

2-3 tablespoons olive oil

4oz/125g chorizo or
other *pimentón* sausage,
sliced

4oz/125g morcilla or
other black pudding,
sliced

1 onion, skinned and
finely chopped

3-4 tomatoes, scalded,
skinned and chopped
(or use canned)

Serves 4-6

The urban poor have long relied on the rich man's left-overs. Triana, Sevilla's old gypsy quarter, is renowned for its flamenco dancers and singers, and bullfighters – and its fine dish of tripe. The main ingredient is most plentiful after the Maestranza, Sevilla's bullring, has hosted a bullfight.

Cut the pre-cooked tripe into 1 inch/2.5 cm squares.

Drain the chickpeas and put them in a large saucepan with the calf's foot or pig's trotter, ham bone or bacon, half the chopped onion, the garlic, parsley and mint sprigs, bay leaf and crushed peppercorns. Cover everything with boiling water and bring to the boil. Cover and cook for 1-1 ½ hours, adding extra boiling water if necessary.

When the chickpeas are soft, stir in the tripe. Remove the calf's foot, carve off the gelatinous meat and return it to the pot. Season, and bring back to a simmer.

Meanwhile, make the *sofrito* (fried flavourings). Warm the olive oil in a frying-pan (skillet) put in the slices of chorizo and morcilla. When they have crisped a little remove and keep warm. Add the remaining onion and fry it gently until it softens and gilds. Add the tomatoes and bubble up, uncovered, for a few minutes to get a rich sauce.

Tip the sauce and the chorizo into the tripe pot, and stir it in. Cook, uncovered, for 15 minutes or so, until the juices look oily and concentrated.

Serve on a shallow dish with the morcilla laid on the top.

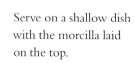

Huevos a la flamenca

Gypsy eggs

4 tablespoons olive oil

1 onion, skinned and chopped

1 garlic clove, skinned and chopped

1 tablespoon chopped parsley

4oz/125g *jamón serrano* cured ham or lean gammon, diced

4oz/125g chorizo or other *pimentón* sausage, thickly sliced

3-4 tomatoes, scalded, skinned and roughly chopped

3 tablespoons green beans, cut into short lengths

3 tablespoons shelled peas

Salt and pepper

4 eggs

Serves 2-4

This must be cooked and served in something resembling a cazuela, a shallow earthenware dish which is flameproof and can be balanced over an open fire. When you buy a new casserole, season it – rub round it with garlic, fill it with water, put it in a hot oven and leave it there until the water has evaporated. Close your eyes and you will see the smoke curling from a gypsy cooking-fire, hear the sharp sound of the pito, *the gypsy whistle which punctuates the dance, smell the sweat of the tired horses, hear the creak of a mule's harness…*

Heat the oil in two flameproof earthenware casseroles. Add the chopped onion and garlic, half to each casserole. Let it soften and take a little colour.

Add the parsley and the meat. Let it fry for a moment, then add the tomatoes. Allow it to bubble up and thicken a little, then stir in the beans and peas and let them stew until soft. Taste, and season with salt and pepper.

Crack two eggs into each dish. Cover loosely as best you can and cook on the top of the stove for about 5 minutes, until the eggs are set. Alternatively, put the dishes in the oven and back at 450°F, 230°C, Gas Mark 8 for about 5 minutes to set the egg whites.

Serve immediately – the beauty of the dish is that the eggs should still be cooking as you set them out, and the yolk can be stirred into the hot vegetables.

Pato a la sevillana

Duck with orange

1 domestic duck,
   or 2 wild ones, jointed
Salt and pepper
2 tablespoons olive oil
4oz/125g bacon,
   cut into cubes
2 garlic cloves, skinned
   and chopped
1 teaspoon ground
   cinnamon
½ teaspoon ground
   cloves
3 tablespoons green
   olives
1 glass white wine
1–2 oranges (depending
   on the size)

Serves 4–6

The wetlands south of Sevilla attract all manner of over-wintering duck, once a great attraction for the hunters. Nowadays, however, most of the vast delta of the Guadalquivir is a nature reserve. In the early spring and autumn, rosy skeins of migrating flamingo thread the flights of teal and wigeon, mallard and pintail as they pass over the busy streets of the city, their calls easily audible above the noise of the traffic.

Wipe the duck joints and season them with salt and pepper. Heat the oil in a flameproof earthenware casserole and add the bacon cubes. Let them fry until the fat runs and browns a little. Put in the duck joints and chopped garlic, and let them fry and take a little colour. Add the spices and the olives. Pour in the wine and let it all bubble up.

Finely grate the zest from the oranges and add it to the casserole. Cover and leave to simmer gently for 30–40 minutes, until the duck is tender.

Peel the oranges right down to the flesh and either slice them, or cut out the segments. Add the pieces to the sauce when you are ready to serve the duck.

A salad of *escarola* (frizzy endive) and chopped onions sprinkled with lemon or bitter orange juice, olive oil, salt and a few tarragon leaves will refresh the palate, Sevilla-style.

Patatas al montón
Heaped potatoes

1½lb/750g potatoes
(allow 1 large potato
per egg)
Salt and pepper
4-6 tablespoons olive oil
1 thick slice Spanish
onion, skinned and
finely chopped
1 garlic clove, skinned
and sliced
4 eggs
1 tablespoon chopped
parsley

*Serves 4 as a starter,
2 as a main course*

*This is a quick and easy dish – halfway between scrambled eggs
with potatoes and a thick potato omelette (tortilla). And it is
perfect for a summer picnic – maybe a romería, pilgrimage, to a
rural Virgin's shrine. No self-respecting Andaluz would dream of
taking only cold food on a day out in the countryside: at least one
hot dish prepared over a little brush fire is a matter of honour.*

Peel and dice the potatoes. Salt them – this really makes a
considerable difference to the flavour, although if the
potatoes have been overfertilized, it *does* make the water run,
and you will need to leave them in a sieve to drain a little.

Put the oil to heat in a small omelette pan. Fry the potatoes,
onion and garlic gently in the oil. Cook the potatoes until
they are quite soft, but are only lightly gilded.

Transfer the potato and onion to a sieve placed over a bowl to
catch the drippings of oil.

Lightly whisk the eggs with the parsley, salt and pepper. Add
the drained potatoes. Pour most of the oil out of the pan,
leaving only 1-2 tablespoons. Return the pan to the heat and
tip in the egg and potato mixture. Fry gently, forking the
mixture over to scramble the eggs. While the mixture is still
nice and juicy, take it off the fire and serve it.

If you get it wrong and the mixture sets, no
matter. Turn it over, fry the other side
and pretend you *always* meant to
make a *tortilla!*

Berza de acelgas

Pork and beans with chard

8oz/250g lean pork,
  cut into cubes
1 tablespoon *pimentón*
1 teaspoon ground
  nutmeg
1 teaspoon chopped
  marjoram
Salt and pepper
8oz/250g pork belly
8oz/250g white haricot
  beans, soaked for a few
  hours or overnight
2 pints/1.2 litres/5 cups
  water
4oz/100g chorizo or
  other *pimentón* sausage
1 tablespoon lard
1lb/500g chard or
  spinach, rinsed and
  roughly chopped
4oz/100g morcilla
  or other black pudding,
  sliced (optional)

Serves 4-6

This is a slow-simmered dish from the Isla Menor. Once water-girt by the river Guadalquivir, the island was a Viking stronghold in the ninth century. The warriors berthed their longships and settled down to sacking the countryside of Sevilla at their leisure. When finally ousted by the forces of the Córdoba-based caliph Abdul-Rahman II, the few survivors embraced Islam and settled down to a bit of back-home dairy farming. The island is still known for its cheeses.

Turn the pork cubes with the spices, marjoram, salt and pepper, and leave them to absorb the flavours.

Put the pork belly and the drained beans in a large saucepan with the water. Bring to the boil, turn down the heat, cover loosely and cook for 1–2 hours, until the beans are soft but not mushy.

Stir in the marinated meat, the chorizo and the lard. Add extra boiling water if necessary and bring everything back to the boil. Stir in the chard or spinach and bring back to the boil. Cover loosely and simmer for 30 minutes or so, until the meat is tender and the juices nearly all absorbed. Taste and season. If you are including morcilla, lay the slices over the top to heat in the steam for the last 10 minutes.

Serve the stew in deep dishes, each with a slice of pork belly and a piece of chorizo. Eat it with a spoon and plenty of bread to push and mop. This is good peasant stuff. Finish the meal with a slice of melon and a piece of Viking-recipe cheese.

Pestino de pichón

Pigeon pie

For the filling

Meat from 2 pigeons, stripped from the bone and finely chopped (leaving the breast fillets in long slivers)

1 teaspoon ground cinnamon

½ teaspoon ground nutmeg

½ teaspoon ground cloves

1 tablespoon raisins, soaked in 1 small glass sherry

1 teaspoon sugar

Salt and pepper

2 tablespoons olive oil

1 garlic clove, skinned and chopped

½ onion, chopped

1 tablespoon pine kernels or slivered almonds

1 raw egg, lightly forked

1 hard-boiled egg, peeled and sliced

For the oil pastry

10oz/300g/2½ cups plain (all-purpose) flour

½ teaspoon salt

1 teaspoon ground cinnamon

4 tablespoons olive oil

2 tablespoons white wine

¼ pint/150ml/⅔ cup milk or water

Serves 6–8

The Moors left plenty of culinary evidence of their seven centuries of residence, including a taste for eastern spices and sweet-and-sour flavourings. This is a descendent of the bestilla *of the Moroccan kitchen.*

Put all the pigeon meat in a bowl with the spices, the raisins and the sherry, sugar, salt and pepper. Heat the oil in a small frying-pan (skillet). Fry the garlic and onion gently for 10 minutes. Add it to the bowl and work in the nuts and egg.

To make the pastry, sieve the flour, salt and cinnamon into a bowl. Put the oil, wine and milk or water into a small pan and heat it to blood temperature. Pour the liquid into the flour, and work together until you have a smooth elastic dough. You may need more liquid or more flour.

Divide the dough into two pieces, one a little larger than the other. Roll each piece out thinly and transfer the smaller one to a greased baking sheet. Spread half the filling over the pastry, leaving a rim, then lay on the slices of hard-boiled egg, and spread on the remainder of the filling.

Cover with the second, larger round of pastry and press the edges together with a fork. Prick the pie all over. Bake in the oven at 400°F, 200°C, Gas Mark 6 for 30 minutes, until the pastry is golden, then turn the heat down to 350°F, 180°C, Gas Mark 4 and cook for another 30 minutes, until the filling is cooked and the pastry nicely browned and firm. Serve hot or cold, accompanied by a glass of *oloroso*.

Mostachos de Utrera

Sponge whiskers

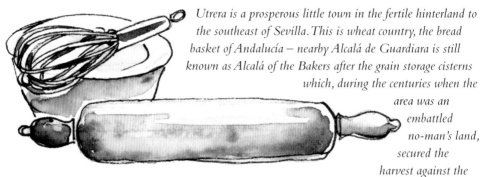

Utrera is a prosperous little town in the fertile hinterland to the southeast of Sevilla. This is wheat country, the bread basket of Andalucía – nearby Alcalá de Guardiara is still known as Alcalá of the Bakers after the grain storage cisterns which, during the centuries when the area was an embattled no-man's land, secured the harvest against the raids of Muslims and Christians alike.

6 eggs, separated
8oz/250g/1¼ cups caster
(superfine) sugar
4oz/125g/1 cup plain
(all-purpose) flour
1 teaspoon ground
cinnamon

Makes about 24 biscuits

Whether Saracen's whiskers or Spanish mostachos, *these deliciously light sponge biscuits* (bizcochos) *are just right for dipping in a glass of honey-sweet dessert wine,* vino dulce.

Whisk the egg whites until firm. Whisk in the sugar slowly, and beat until you have a stiff meringue. Whisk in the egg yolks. Sieve the flour with the cinnamon, and gently fold it into the egg and sugar mixture with a metal spoon.

Line a baking sheet with greased paper. Using a tablespoon, drop on double dollops of the mixture, in the shape of a handlebar moustache.

Bake in the oven at 400°F, 200°C, Gas Mark 6 for 10 minutes, until crisp and golden. Peel off the paper and transfer the whiskers to a wire rack to cool.

THE FLAVOURS OF ANDALUCÍA

Tortas de aceite

Olive oil biscuits

12oz/350g/3 cups strong white (all-purpose) flour
1½ teaspoons ground cinnamon
¾ pint/150ml/⅔ cup olive oil
A strip of lemon peel
1 teaspoon grated lemon zest
1½ teaspoons sesame seeds
1½ teaspoons fennel seeds
3floz/75ml/⅓ cup white wine or water
3 tablespoons sugar
1 tablespoon slivered almonds

Makes 24 biscuits

Crisp round biscuits, blistered black from the first heat of the bread oven, are the traditional Sevillan breakfast – perfect for dipping in a cup of the hot chocolate Columbus's heirs brought back from the Americas. Naturally, they compete with the ubiquitous dough-fritter fryers for the morning custom.

Sieve the flour into a bowl and mix in the cinnamon. Put the oil to heat in a pan with the strip of lemon peel. When it boils, take it off the heat, leave it for a moment, then remove the peel and stir in the sesame and fennel seeds.

When the oil cools, mix in the wine or water, the grated lemon zest and the sugar. Pour this mixture into a well in the flour and work it all into a soft dough. Leave it to rest for about 30 minutes.

Divide the dough into 24 pieces, work each into a ball and roll it out into a thin biscuit. Transfer the biscuits to an oiled baking sheet and sprinkle with the almond slivers.

Bake the biscuits in the oven at 450°F, 230°C, Gas Mark 8, until they blister and crisp – about 6-8 minutes, depending on the thickness of the dough and the capacity of your oven. You may need to dry them out in a low oven later if you want to store them for any length of time.

Isla flotante

Floating island

This is a favourite among the sherry-producing families of Jérez, whose close ties with their best customers, the British, is evident in the Anglo-Saxon names many of them bear. In addition, generations of English nannies instilled in their young Spanish charges a taste for English nursery food, including such childhood staples as rice pudding and prunes and custard. This is the grown-up version of these solid dishes.

Whisk together the egg yolks, 1 tablespoon of the sugar, the milk and the cream in a heatproof bowl. Add the vanilla pod or whisk in the essence.

6 eggs, separated
10oz/300g/1¼ cups caster (superfine) sugar
1 pint/600ml/2½ cups milk
½ pint/300ml/1¼ cups single (light) cream
1 small vanilla pod, or a few drops vanilla essence
2-3 tablespoons orange liqueur or brandy (optional)

Serves 6-8

Settle the bowl over a pan of simmering water and keep stirring until the mixture thickens enough to coat the back of the spoon. Should it curdle, process it in the blender or food processor for a moment with a splash of cold milk.

Meanwhile, whisk the egg whites until well frothed and firm, adding the sugar gradually until you have a stiff meringue. Remove the bowl of custard from the pan, and let it cool a little. Remove the vanilla pod, whisk in the orange liqueur or brandy, if using, and pour it all into a pretty glass bowl.

Float spoonfuls of the meringue mixture on the simmering water and poach them for a few minutes until they set. Remove them carefully with a slotted spoon and slip them onto the custard as floating islands.

Naranjas en mermelada
Marmaladed oranges

12 marmalade oranges
1½ oz/40g/3 tablespoons sugar

Serves 4

The eponymous orange of Sevilla is the marmalade orange, so bitter it is unpalatable raw, but delicious when well sugared. The fruit of the orange trees whose blossom scents the graceful squares of the city are mostly naranjas de cañja, *sugarcane oranges, lacking in the acidity that gives the fruit its bite. This may account for the lack of interest taken in the crop by the city's urchins, who are otherwise more than capable of stripping a car of its saleable parts in a few minutes.*

Squeeze the juice from six of the oranges and strain it through a fine sieve. Wash and peel the other six right down so that the pith is all cut off, then cut the flesh into slices. Layer the slices in a casserole, sprinkling sugar between the layers. Pour in the orange juice.

Cover and either simmer on the top of the stove, if the casserole is a flameproof one, for about 15 minutes, or bake in the oven at 350°F, 180°C, Gas Mark 4 for 20-30 minutes.

Serve cool – they are lovely with vanilla ice cream.

Magdalenas de Castilleja
Madeleines

4 eggs
8oz/250g/1 cup sugar
8floz/250ml/1 cup
   olive oil (some cooks
   heat this to frying
   temperature and cool
   it before using it,
   so the olive taste is not
   so strong)
8oz/250g/1 cup plain
   (all-purpose) flour
Grated zest of ½ lemon

Makes 24 madeleines

The pastrycooks of Castilleja de la Costa are famous in Sevilla. These magdalenas *are a speciality of the 'Irish' Convent, the Instituto de la Virgen Buenaventura. Sweet cakes were always the tribute due on the Virgin's feast days. The little town's other claim to fame is that it was the chosen retirement home of Conquistador Hernán Cortés, Marquis of Oaxaca. Cortés's bones were shipped out to Mexico, but his horse, Star, was permitted to rest here in the convent.*

Whisk the eggs with the sugar until the mixture is light, white and absolutely fluffy. (This takes longer than you think, so keep going.)

Whisk in the oil gradually. Finally, fold in the flour and the grated lemon zest.

Drop tablespoons of the mixture into 24 well-greased madeleine or sponge-finger tins (pans) – you should fill them two-thirds full.

Bake the *magdalenas* in the oven at 375°F, 190°C, Gas Mark 5 for 15-20 minutes, until they are well risen and a nice golden-brown colour.

Yemas de San Leandro

Saint Leandro's yolks

For the yolk-threads
14-18 egg yolks
   (they should weigh
   9oz/275g), absolutely
   free of any white
1lb/500g/2 cups sugar
½ pint/300ml/1¼ cups
   water

For the fondant
A few drops lemon juice
2 egg whites

Makes about 18 yemas

This is a marvellously tricky recipe, requiring not only the patience of a saint, but also a special instrument which looks like a miniature metal udder, through which to trickle the egg yolk into the boiling syrup. Any ironmonger in Sevilla will have the instrument – ask for an embudo de cinco pitor-ritos para yemas. *You can get the same effect – although in five times the time – with a fine icing pipe. Dollops of the sweet yolk-threads are coated in thin fondant icing. Try it on a rainy day – and keep your fingers out of the boiling syrup.*

Strain the egg yolks (you can make meringues with all the whites) through a fine-meshed sieve to remove any threads and solids (ideally, the sieve should be warm – pour boiling water through it and let it dry by the side of the stove).

In a saucepan (one on which you can rest the *embudo* if you have one), make a syrup with the water and sugar. Start slowly, stirring until the granules dissolve, and then boil it until it registers 240°F, 120°C on a sugar thermometer.

Trickle in the egg yolk in a very fine stream (using the *embudo* or a fine icing nozzle). The yolk will set as it hits the hot syrup. Do not let the syrup come off a gently bubbling boil.

When all the egg yolk has been trickled in (you may need to do it in more than one go) lift the hank of threads out carefully with a slotted spoon, and put it to drain in a colander, catching the drippings in a basin placed underneath. As soon as the threads have cooled a little (they should still be damp) drop yolk-sized pyramids of them into paper cases.

Sieve the syrup drippings back into the pan, stir in a few drops of lemon juice, and bring the syrup back to the boil. Meanwhile, beat the two egg whites until quite stiff. When the syrup has reached 240°F, 120°C, take it off the heat and as soon as the bubbles subside, pour it in a thin stream onto the egg whites, still whisking vigorously – you'll need →

an electric whisk or another pair of hands for this. Beat the fondant as it cools. When it starts to look dull it is well on the way to setting, so pour it quickly over the yolk threads.

Accompany these rich little mouthfuls with a glass of cold water, Moorish-style, and a tiny cup of strong black coffee.

Polvorónes sevillanos
Dusty biscuits

8oz/250g lard

8oz/250g/1¼ cups caster (superfine)sugar

2 egg yolks

Grated zest of 1 lemon

1lb/500g/4 cups plain (all-purpose) flour, sieved

8oz/250g/2¼ cups ground almonds

1 tablespoon ground cinnamon

Lemon juice (optional)

Makes about 24 biscuits

These cinnamon and almond biscuits, the Christmas treat all over Spain, are most likely of Arab origin – although the use of pork lard makes them food for infidels. This recipe comes from Estepa, not far outside Sevilla on the dusty road to Granada. The town is as famous for the dust it kicked up while resisting the besieging Roman, Scipio Africanus, as it is for the excellence of its dusty biscuits.

Soften the lard and whisk it with the sugar, egg yolks and lemon zest until fluffy. Beat in the sieved flour, ground almonds and cinnamon until you have a soft dough. Add a little lemon juice if wished.

Roll out the dough to the thickness of a thumb, and cut out rounds with a small wineglass. Transfer the biscuits to a greased baking tray.

Bake the biscuits in the oven at 400°F, 200°C, Gas Mark 6 for 15-20 minutes, and then turn the oven down to 350°F, 180°C, Gas Mark 4 and cook for another 15-20 minutes until they are pale gold. Carefully transfer them to a wire rack to cool – they are very crumbly.

When cool, wrap each biscuit in a scrap of tissue paper and store in an airtight tin. Tuck a couple in the shoe of your favourite child on 6 January, the time when all good Andalucían children hope to share the good fortune of the Christ Child on the day he was visited by the Three Kings.

Huelva

THE PROVINCE OF HUELVA stretches north to take in the
mountains of the Sierra Morena; its southernmost reaches consist
mostly of coastal plain, including much of the delta of the
Guadalquivir and the long sandy littoral which borders it. This
plain stretches from the Coto Doñana across to Palos de la
Frontera, the supplier of Christopher Columbus's ships and sailors,
and its neighbouring Monastery of La Rábida which offered the
navigator a safe house while he attempted to loosen the purse
strings of the Catholic Kings, Ferdinand and Isabel. Columbus's
search for a new spice route was to have gastronomic conse-
quences far greater than the supply of luxuries: the importation
of New World vegetables, including staples such as potatoes and
maize, had so dramatic an effect on the diet of Europe that it can
be held responsible for the population explosions of the eighteenth century, which provided the manpower that fuelled the
industrial and social revolutions of modern times.

In the sandy basin of the Guadalquivir, too, is the sleepy cross-roads town of Almonte, stranded amongst vines and sand-rooted clumps of alien eucalyptus. A few miles further towards the ocean, through the shoulder-high scrub of the Coto Doñana, is the sanctuary of Almonte's patroness, the Virgen del Rodo, Our Lady of the Dew. For most of the year Almonte goes about its business quietly. Down the road, the white village of Rocío is deserted; the broad unpaved streets, lined with hitching rails for horses, have the look of a Hollywood western after the posse has gone home. But for one week of the year at Whitsuntide, Almonte's crossroads are one long traffic jam, and Rocío is swamped by thousands of pilgrims anxious to pay their respects to the Sin Peca'o – the Sinless One – whose fame reaches far beyond the boundaries of Andalucía, and who chose to hang her shepherd-ess's hat and halo here in the thirteenth century.

It was the men of Almonte who found the grave-faced little wooden Virgin under a thicket after the Moors had been driven out, and she miraculously refused to be moved from her chosen spot. The Lady's reputation as a worker of miracles spread, and brotherhoods of pilgrims began to visit her at Whitsuntide from as far away as Sevilla and Cádiz. These days her festival, once the privilege of those horsemen, waggoners and foot pilgrims who took long days and nights to ford the rivers and scale the dunes, is open to all who care to take the new road which bisects Almonte. And thousands take it, by the bus-load. The pilgrimage is a merry one, well soused with sherry wine and provisioned with the good ham of the mountains. In the thronged bridleways of Rocío itself,

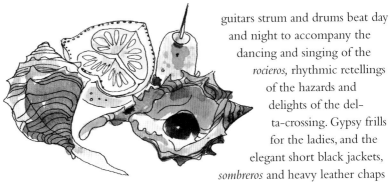

guitars strum and drums beat day and night to accompany the dancing and singing of the *rocieros,* rhythmic retellings of the hazards and delights of the delta-crossing. Gypsy frills for the ladies, and the elegant short black jackets, *sombreros* and heavy leather chaps of the Andaluz horsemen are still required dress for those who wish to honour the Virgin, the White Dove of the Dew.

The coastline of Huelva, the Costa de la Luz, is fringed with long wind-swept beaches, their fine pale sand kept clean by the rolling breakers of the Atlantic. Columbus felt the force of their buffeting when, on his return from his first voyage, the whole of western Europe was lashed by hurricane storms. The navigator took shelter in the lee of Huelva under the protection of Santa Maria de la Cinta, the Virgin of the Girdle. The patron saint of seamen seems to have inherited the wardrobe as well as the responsibilities of the goddess Aphrodite, who once cast her own magic girdle to quieten these same waves. The anteroom to the Pillars of Hercules is no stranger to storms, and the fishermen of Huelva take advantage of the rich harvest of sea-creatures which, like Columbus's *Niña* are driven to take shelter in the estuaries and inlets of the Odiel and the Guadiana.

Huelva's port, sheltered by the Island of Saltes (once time-shared by Viking raiders and local metalworkers), now handles a proportion of Spain's export of chemicals. The cookery of the province's littoral has much in common with that of neighbouring Cádiz – fishy stews, made with anything and everything that swam into the nets of the fishermen, whose main business is keeping the sardine and tuna-canning factories supplied. The fleets sail out of the frontier town of Ayamonte – to Portugal, just a short ferry-ride across the estuary of the Guadiana, and to the Isla Cristina, not an island at all, but joined to the mainland by a long narrow peninsula. The canning industry is the descendent of the salting and barrelling trades which were the hallmark of all ship-provisioning ports.

As well as from its fish-canning industry and its adventurous sailors, Huelva's wealth came from the mining area of Rio Tinto in the mountains behind. Huelva also has her mountains to thank for the marvellous salt-cured hams of Jabugo, a sombre little town cradled in the Sierra Morena, its landscape more like that of Extremadura than Andalucía. The pigs of the semi-wild reddish Iberian breed, which yield the lean 'black' hams (the prized *pata negra*), are traditionally fattened up on acorns from the surrounding forests, and are turned out to glean in the woods during the autumn. EEC regulations are making such freedoms difficult, so we may be seeing the last of the true wild foraging pig. Nevertheless, the draughty rafters of Jabugo are hung through the winter with a forest of salt-frosted hams, many of them sent up for curing in the cold dry mountain air by cousins or relatives who farm too close to the warm, damp sea air of the littoral to cure their own. As with the hams of Trevelez, the raw-cured *jamón serrano* of Jabugo is best savoured in paper-thin slices, not in cubes like the hams of La Mancha. The best bit, to my taste, is the long fillet from underneath the animal, carved in long, slender, translucent slices, like dark crimson velvet. Everything is edible – the rind, fat trimmings and sawn-up bones all enrich the slow-simmered stews of winter.

If fishing and sailing are the activities of the coast, cork-oak forestry is the industry of the mountains. The silver-limbed evergreens yield three crops. The most profitable is the cork-bark itself, still the best way to keep air out of a wine bottle: this is the landlord's share, cropped every seven to nine years by gangs of strippers engaged seasonally, like sheepshearers. The cork is one of the outer layers of bark, and is stripped off up to the height of a man, leaving the coppery inner bark exposed on

the lower trunk, but with the upper branches still shimmering silver, like debutantes with their arms thrust into long pale gloves. The trees offer two subsidiary crops, not so profitable but contributing rather more to the wellbeing of the native inhabitants. One of these is the fine fat acorns, *bellotas*, on which the red pigs feed. The pigs know a good thing when they snout it out; humans also like nibbling fresh *bellotas*, and the green nuts are to be found on sale in the market during the autumn. The second crop is the wood used for charcoal, which, in these cold uplands, still provides isolated rural households with fuel for cooking and heating. Many country people keep warm in winter by means of the *mesa camelia,* a small round table equipped with a charcoal brazier beneath and a floor-length round blanket over the top. It's a primitive form of spot-heating; family and friends sit around the table sipping a glass of wine, with the communal blanket over their knees and their lower limbs snug in the warmth beneath – deliciously effective and very convivial. Many a courtship has been conducted round the *mesa camelia,* in full view of the prospective in-laws.

Jabugo does not appear to cater to visitors. When I visited it a few years ago, it was hard to find even a slice of ham in the single road-side bar. The deficiency is rectified down the road in Aracena, whose famous stalagmited caves are a favourite day trip on hot summer Sundays for the citizens of Huelva, Sevilla and even Cádiz looking for a little respite from the dusty plains of the coast. There are good restaurants catering to this native tourism. In the spring, you may see small boys on the road selling grass-tied bundles of slender green mountain asparagus, gathered in the lavender-scented maquis beneath the tall bushes of a cistus whose crumpled white blossoms centered with burgundy markings proclaim it to be the gum-yielding *Cistus ladanifer.* This plant, its common name labdano, was known to the Moors, Romans, Greeks, and all the way back to the Ancient Persians, for its aromatic milky juices used in scent-making.

Huelva, gatekeeper to the highways of the Atlantic, has had no shortage of visitors over the centuries. The contents of her cooking pot reflect her trade.

Caldereta con castañas
Bean-pot with chestnuts

6oz/175g white haricot beans, soaked for a few hours or overnight

2oz/50g *jamón serrano* cured ham trimmings, including the rich yellow fat (or 4oz/125g bacon bits)

2 tablespoons olive oil

3 carrots, scraped and cut into chunks

1 onion, skinned and chopped

2 garlic cloves, left in their skins and singed in a flame

1 bay leaf

1 short cinnamon stick

2-3 cloves

6 white peppercorns, crushed

4oz/125g dried chestnuts, soaked for a few hours, or canned chestnuts in brine

2-3 links chorizo or other *pimentón* sausage

8oz/250g pumpkin, skinned and diced

1 large potato, peeled and cut into chunks

Salt and pepper

1 tablespoon wine vinegar or bitter orange juice

Serves 4-6

This is a winter stew from Jabugo, a little mountain town whose main business is the curing of hams, preferably those of the scavenging lean red pigs of the old Iberian breed. All around are chestnut groves, planted many decades ago on the slopes of the hills, thus making the cropping relatively easy – the men would go up in the branches and beat out the spike-sheathed nuts which would then roll down the slope for the women and children waiting at the bottom to collect in large white sheets. The crop would either be sold fresh down in the cities of the plain, or dried for winter stews. After the harvest the pigs would be set loose in the woods to glean. This slow-simmered one-pot meal deliciously combines Jabugo's two staples.

Drain the beans. Put all the ingredients, except the chestnuts, chorizo, pumpkin, potato, salt and pepper and vinegar or orange juice, in a large pan.

Pour in enough water to submerge everything to a depth of two fingers. Bring to the boil, cover and turn down the heat. Let it simmer gently for about 1 hour, then drain the chestnuts and add them to the pan. Cook for a further hour or so, until the beans are perfectly tender.

Check that the pot doesn't boil dry, and add extra boiling water if necessary. When the beans are tender, add the chorizo, the pumpkin and potato, bring all back to the boil and cook for 20 minutes or so, until the vegetables are tender.

Taste and add salt and pepper. Stir in the wine vinegar or bitter orange juice and serve.

Gazpacho caliente

Hot gazpacho

8oz/250g day-old bread
5 tablespoons olive oil
1 red pepper, hulled,
   de-seeded and
   cut into strips
2 garlic cloves, skinned
   and finely chopped
1 tablespoon wine
   vinegar or bitter
   orange juice
2½ pints/1.5 litres/
   6¼ cups chicken or
   game stock, or water
1 large tomato, chopped
1 small cucumber, diced
1 hard-boiled egg, peeled
   and sliced
2oz/50g *jamón serrano*
   cured ham or gammon,
   diced

Serves 4

The thick peasant gazpachos of Andalucía have little in common with the delicately chilled tomato soup of international fame. Andaluz housewives were turning their leftover bread into bread-porridges long before the arrival of upstart New World vegetables such as tomatoes and peppers, although there's no doubt they improve the flavour. Use the best bread – pan macho, rough-milled, whole, unbleached country bread – to appreciate why these dishes are so much enjoyed. Plain water is for every day, chicken stock is a treat, and game stock is the height of luxury.

Cube the bread into a large bowl – save the crumbs.

In a large saucepan, fry the pepper strips in a little of the olive oil until they soften and caramelize. Add the garlic and crush it into the hot oil with the leftover breadcrumbs. When it has fried a little, work in the vinegar or orange juice, and the remaining oil. Pour in the stock or water, stir well, then bring it all to the boil.

Pour the hot liquid onto the cubed bread and leave it for 10 minutes to soak up the broth. Stir in the chopped tomato and diced cucumber.

Ladle the gazpacho into bowls, and top each helping with a slice or two of egg and a few cubes of ham.

Paella rociera

Pilgrims' paella

1lb/500g Arborio
(round-grain) rice
6-8 tablespoons oil
1 small wild rabbit,
jointed into 16 pieces
1 pigeon or partridge,
jointed
8oz/250g eel, skinned
and chopped into
medallions
2 garlic cloves, skinned
and chopped
1 green pepper, hulled,
de-seeded and roughly
chopped
8oz/250g tomatoes,
coarsely grated
A handful of asparagus
sprue, chopped into
pea-sized lengths
6 saffron threads, soaked
in a splash of hot water
(or 1 teaspoon ground
saffron)
1 teaspoon salt

Serves 4-6

A proper paella is cooked in the open air, over a wood fire, in a purpose-made, shallow, double-handled iron pan. It is traditionally prepared by the father of the family and is not served in the evening, even on a pilgrimage, but at midday. The same rice dish cooked indoors by a woman is called un arroz, 'a rice'. The distinctive 'ingredient' is the cooking pan, the design of which is based on the Roman patella, and which needs a wide spread of even heat to allow the rice to cook in a single layer. These days you can buy special gas rings with a very wide circle of jets for making a paella in the kitchen – but even so, this is really a restaurant trick. It is a dish along the line of the Italian risotto, with the flavouring ingredients cooked in with the rice so the juices are all absorbed. The basis is round-grained rice, saffron and olive oil – the rest of the ingredients are highly variable, with ingredients gathered as much as possible from the wild. This version is made with wild game and eel from the marshes and dunes, and the native wild asparagus sprue which is gathered in the scrub.

Pick over the rice. Heat a *paella* pan or a wide frying-pan (skillet), and pour in the oil. When it is lightly hazed with smoke, put in the rabbit and pigeon or partridge pieces, turning and frying them on all sides. Then add the eel pieces, the garlic, and the chopped pepper and fry them for a few minutes. Add the rice and turn it in the oil until all the grains are coated and transparent.

Finally, add the tomatoes, the chopped asparagus sprue and the saffron with its soaking water, then pour in as much water as will cover the rice and meats – the volume of liquid to rice is 2:1, so if you measure the rice into the pan with a cup, you can add two cups of water for every one of rice. Add the salt.

Let the *paella* cook for 20 minutes in all, pouring in more hot water if the moisture evaporates too quickly (it should still be visibly moist when you take it off the heat). If cooking on an open charcoal fire, let it rest, covered by a cloth, for 10 minutes – this gives the rice time to finish swelling and the grains to separate. If you're cooking the *paella* on a gas or electric stove, you will have to keep the rice moving as it cooks and you do not need to give it the resting period.

Almost any combination of shellfish and meat will taste good. I have had *paella*s made with crayfish, squid, chicken, mussels, clams, pork, even black pudding and snails, all of them delicious.

Serve the *paella* in its pan – setting it down in the middle of the table and providing each of your guests with a fork and a piece of bread for pushing. The traditional way to eat a *paella* is straight out of the pan, with each person tackling the portion directly in front of him or her.

Chocos con habas

Cuttlefish with broad beans

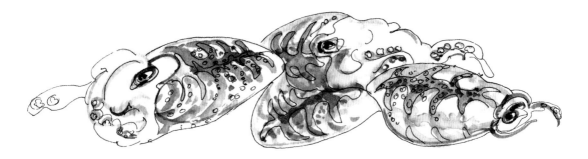

1lb/500g cuttlefish
2 tablespoons olive oil
2 garlic cloves, skinned
   and chopped
Salt and pepper
8oz/250g shelled broad
   beans
1 glass dry sherry
1 glass water
1 teaspoon chopped
   oregano or marjoram

Serves 3-4

The fishermen of Huelva prize cuttlefish above their prettier cousin the squid, finding them more tender and with a more delicate flavour. You can tell the difference quite easily: cuttlefish are round-bodied and their 'bone' is that chalky cuttle much appreciated by caged birds; the squid has a longer cone-shaped body and its 'bone' looks as if it's made of clear plastic. Generically the cuttlefish is smaller — although if you have large examples of one and small of the other, identification is harder. You can use squid for this recipe if you prefer, and frozen broad beans can be used if you cannot get hold of fresh ones.

Rinse the cuttlefish and remove the chalky cuttle (budgies and canaries love it) and soft innards from the tentacles and body. Discard the innards and the eyes and chop up the rest. If the cuttlefish are large, you will need to scrape the little 'toenails' off the tentacles.

Heat the oil in a shallow flameproof earthenware casserole (*cazuela de barro*) or a heavy frying-pan (skillet). Add the garlic and let it soften. Slip in the cuttlefish and let it cook gently in the oil and its own juices, seasoned with salt and pepper, for about 10 minutes. Add the beans, the sherry and the water and let it all bubble up. Sprinkle in the chopped oregano or marjoram, cover with the lid and let it cook gently for 20 minutes or so, until the cuttlefish is tender.

Remove the lid, turn up the heat and bubble it up until there is only a slick of oily juices left. Serve with chunks of bread for mopping juices and wiping fingers.

Centolla al coñac
Spider crab with brandy

Salted water (6oz/175g
 of salt to 4 pints/
 2 litres/10 cups water)
1 live spider crab, or
 1 large cooked crab
8 tablespoons olive oil
2 garlic cloves, skinned
 and sliced
1 green chilli, de-seeded
 and chopped, or
 1 teaspoon cayenne
2 tablespoons brandy

Serves 4

The spider crab, maja squinado, *is a spiky, scarlet creature with such weak claws it avoids predators by draping its rough carapace with a seaweed camouflage. It tastes excellent – although of course you can use any crabmeat in this recipe. If using a live crab, it should still be alive when you cook it, as crabmeat blackens immediately once the animal is dead. As a crab throws its legs off if plunged into boiling water, I start with cold water and bring it slowly to the boil, hoping this lulls the creature to sleep.*

Fill a large saucepan with the heavily-salted water, put in the live crab and hold it under for 2 minutes. Bring it slowly to the boil, then turn down the heat, and keep it just on the boil for 20 minutes or so, depending on the size of the creature.

Drain the crab, pull the body a little away from the shell, and prop it up to drain and cool, and for the meat to set.

Pull the body away from the shell and cut off the feathery grey lungs and mouthpiece. Chop off each leg, angling the knife towards the body to divide the crab into ten 'lollipops'. Pick off all the meat and mix it with the dark body meat.

Put the olive oil to heat in a shallow flameproof casserole or heavy frying-pan (skillet). Add the garlic and let it take a little colour, then stir in the chopped chilli (if using cayenne, don't let it fry). Stir in the crabmeat and brandy and turn up the heat. Sprinkle with a little salt and bring the mixture to a rapid boil. Fry the crab for as little time as possible to preserve its flavour.

Serve very hot as soon as the alcohol has evaporated, with quartered lemons and chunks of bread to mop up the juices.

Caldereta de Almonte

Pilgrims' lamb

**2lb/1kg young lamb or
  kid, cut into chunks
  across the bone**
**1 tablespoon seasoned
  flour**
3 tablespoons olive oil
**1 tablespoon chopped
  raw ham, or gammon**
**1 large onion, skinned
  and chopped**
**2-3 garlic cloves, skinned
  and chopped**
**2 tablespoons chopped
  parsley**
1-2 rosemary sprigs
1-2 sage leaves
1-2 thyme sprigs
6 peppercorns, crushed
**1 glass dry sherry or
  white wine**
1 glass water
Salt

Serves 4

*This is the dish the pilgrims of Almonte prepare over a low fire
when they sleep under the stars on their annual visit to the shrine
of their patroness. There is no more certain absolution for the year's
sins than keeping the Whitsun vigil with the Mother of God.*

Toss the meat in the seasoned flour.

Heat the oil in a shallow flameproof earthenware casserole or
heavy frying-pan (skillet), and add the chopped ham or
gammon, onion and garlic. Let it fry gently for a few minutes.
Add the herbs and peppercorns.

Put in the meat chunks and turn them in the hot oil. Let the
meat caramelize a little. Splash in the sherry or wine and the
water. Bubble it all up, sprinkle in a little salt, turn down the
heat, put the lid on loosely and let it simmer *very* gently for 1
hour or so, until the meat is falling off the bone. Add extra hot
water if necessary.

Accompany with bread and a glass of chilled dry sherry.

Rosas del Rocío

Roses of the dew

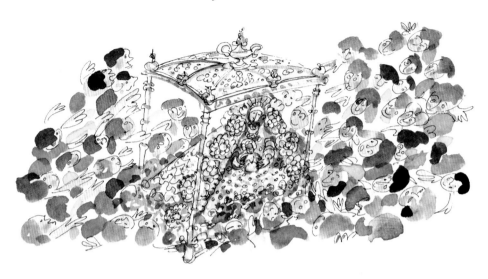

12 eggs
¼ pint/150ml/⅔ cup
   olive oil
6oz/175g/1½ cups plain
   (all-purpose) flour,
   sieved
1 small glass anisette
   (aguardiente), **or vodka**
   with 1 teaspoon
   aniseed added
Oil for frying

To finish
8oz/250g/⅔ cup clear
   honey
2 tablespoons toasted
   sesame seeds

Makes about 24 fritters

The Mother of God is courted with sweet things – and this little honeyed treat is made to celebrate the Virgin of the Dew's special day. The roses should really be made with a special implement like a branding iron in the shape of a flower, which is first heated in the oil, then dipped into the batter, then thrust back into the oil and flicked to detach the fritter. However, the batter can be just as easily trickled into the oil without this special implement.

Beat the eggs with an electric whisk until they are light and fluffy (if hand-powered, you would need to beat for about 1 hour!). Beat in the oil. Fold in the flour and then the anisette or vodka. Leave it to rest for 30 minutes.

Heat a deep panful of oil until it is hot enough to fry a cube of bread golden instantly. Using a ladle, drop curls of batter on to the surface of the oil – only a few at a time so that the oil temperature doesn't drop. When the fritters are crisp and golden, remove and drain them on kitchen paper. Continue until all the batter has been used.

Warm the honey and trickle it over the fritters. Finish with a sprinkling of toasted sesame seeds.

Perdices con piñones

Partridges with pine kernels

4 tablespoons olive oil
**2 partridges, cleaned and
  neatly jointed**
2oz/50g raw ham, diced
1 tablespoon pine kernels
**1 large onion, skinned
  and chopped**
**8 garlic cloves, left in
  their skins**
2 glasses water
**2 tablespoons sherry
  or wine vinegar**
Pinch of ground saffron
1 bay leaf, torn
2-3 cloves
**1lb/500g potatoes, peeled
  and cut into chunks**

Serves 4

*The Andaluz takes no risks with his game – whether tender young
hen or scrawny old cock, he cooks it until the meat falls off the bone.
The sandy dunes of the Guadalquivir's delta were, until recently, a
hunter's paradise. Now most of this desert of reeds, maquis and
dunes punctuated with out-crops of broad-topped umbrella pines, is
a nature reserve. The rules forbid even the gathering of pine cones.
Cracking open the hard nuts to get at the sweet, cream-coloured
kernels used to keep the children busy for ages.*

Heat the oil in a flameproof earthenware casserole or heavy
saucepan. Put in the partridge joints, ham or bacon, and pine
kernels and turn everything in the hot oil until it begins to
take a little colour.

Add the onion and garlic cloves and fry them for a moment.
Pour in the water and vinegar and sprinkle in the saffron,
torn-up bay leaf and the cloves. Add salt and pepper.

Bring to the boil, turn down the heat, cover tightly and leave
to simmer for 50-60 minutes, until the meat is falling off the
bone, adding the potato chunks after 30 minutes.

Take off the lid towards the end, and evaporate off the juices,
to leave a rich aromatic oil. Take out the partridge joints, turn
up the heat a little more and let the potatoes, which should by
now be quite done, sauté a little.

Serve all together, with bread and a cos lettuce salad to refresh
the palate.

Torta de bellotas

Acorn cake

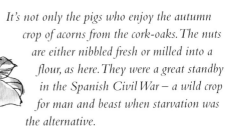

It's not only the pigs who enjoy the autumn crop of acorns from the cork-oaks. The nuts are either nibbled fresh or milled into a flour, as here. They were a great standby in the Spanish Civil War – a wild crop for man and beast when starvation was the alternative.

You can use any nuts for the flour (hazelnuts, for example) instead of acorns.

8oz/250g acorns
4oz/125g/½ cup lard or
   margarine
8oz/250g/1 cup caster
   (superfine) sugar
2 eggs
1 teaspoon ground
   cinnamon
1 teaspoon grated lemon
   zest
1 tablespoon flour

Makes 1 cake

Skin the acorns – treat them as if they were chestnuts: scald them first and then peel them. Dry them thoroughly and grind them to a fine powder in a food processor.

Beat the lard or margarine with the sugar until it is light and fluffy. Beat in the eggs, one by one, and add the cinnamon and lemon zest. Fold in the ground acorns.

Grease a 8 inch/20 cm shallow cake tin (pan) and dust it lightly with flour. Spread the cake mixture in the tin. Bake in the oven at 350°F, 180°C, Gas Mark 4 for 40-50 minutes, until the cake is firm and well browned.

Serve it with a fruit salad (it's good with cream as well, but that's not at all Andaluz).

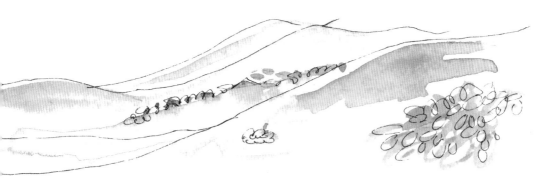

Sandia al ron

Watermelon with rum

1 smallish watermelon,
   or any other type of
   melon
1 small glass rum
1 glass sugar
Juice of 1 lemon

Serves 4–6

In high summer, the parched fields of the province's littoral produce, like a mirage in the desert, a crop of what appears to be huge green billiard balls tethered to the dust. Great pyramids of the green globes, splitting open under the weight of pink flesh and juice, appear in all the markets in midsummer. The children sit in the sunshine and suck the sweet juicy flesh off the ebony-smooth pips, while the adults enjoy this, more grown-up, refreshment – the same fruit, marinated in rum. Rum, sugar cane spirit, has long been available to the natives of the ports that serviced the new Indies.

Cut a neat round lid from the stalk end of the melon. Scoop out all the flesh with whatever implement you prefer – melon-baller, sharp knife, whatever. Cut into chunks, discarding the seeds.

Mix the melon flesh with the rest of the ingredients and return it to the hollow skin. Replace the lid.

Put the melon in the refrigerator for a few hours before serving, so that it is really cold.

Churros con chocolate
Doughnut fritters with hot chocolate sauce

For the fritters
8oz/250g/2 cups plain
(all-purpose) flour
½ pint/300ml/1¼ cups
water
1 tablespoon olive oil
1 teaspoon salt
Oil for frying

For the hot chocolate sauce
1½ pints/900ml/3¾ cups
water
6oz/175g plain
(unsweetened)
chocolate, broken into
small pieces
1 short cinnamon stick
6 tablespoons sweetened
condensed milk

Serves 4

This is the traditional breakfast after a long night's singing, dancing and toasting the Mother of God with dry sherry wine. It fortifies the body and restores the spirit for the long day and night ahead. No one sleeps on the Rocío pilgrimage.

To make the fritters, first sieve the flour. Bring the water, oil and salt to the boil in a large saucepan. When it boils, pour in the flour all at once. Stir it in and then beat it over the heat for a few minutes until you have a smooth paste. Leave to cool completely.

Heat a deep panful of oil until it is hot enough to fry a cube of bread golden instantly.

Using either a wide-nozzled biscuit syringe, or one of the special implements available at any Spanish ironmonger, squeeze lengths of the dough in a spiral into the hot oil – not too many at a time, or the oil temperature will drop. If the oil is too hot, the *churros* burst, if it's too cool, they will not be light and airy. Cook until crisp and golden.

Meanwhile, make the hot chocolate sauce. Put the chocolate pieces in a small saucepan with the water and cinnamon stick, and melt gently over a low heat. Stir it every now and then so that it does not stick to the pan. When it is hot and the chocolate dissolved (some like to add a little cornflour to thicken it), fish out and discard the cinnamon, and whisk in the condensed milk.

Using tongs, take out the *churros* and drain on kitchen paper. Serve hot, to dip in the hot chocolate. In the north they like their *churros* sugared, but in Andalucía we like them as they are.

Dulce de cidra

Candied citron

**2lb/1kg citrons, lemons
  or bitter oranges**
2lb/1kg/4 cups sugar
1 short cinnamon stick
A twist of lemon peel

To finish
Icing sugar, for dusting

Makes about 2lb/1kg fruit

This is a traditional wedding treat. Food which combines sweet and sharp, soft and strong flavours frequently features in marriage feasts as a metaphor for the rough and tumble of wedlock. In these more affluent days, candied fruits are a speciality of the fairground and Christmas time as well.

The citron is the Mediterranean's original citrus fruit – the earliest cultivar, it appears, was brought over from the Orient c.300 BC. The elongated yellow-green fruit has a rough skin and plenty of pith, which makes its peel ideal for candying, though lemons or bitter oranges can be substituted.

Wash and scrub the citrons, or other citrus fruit and cut them into chunks – or (more elegant) slice them either vertically or horizontally. Remove the pips.

Put the sugar in a large saucepan (copper is advocated, but this is copper-mining country) and pour in just enough water to submerge the crystals. Bring to the boil gently, stirring so that the sugar dissolves. Let it froth, turn down the heat and skim off the foam.

Add the citron pieces, bring back to the boil and simmer gently for 25-30 minutes, until the peel is tender. Remove each piece delicately with a slotted spoon and set it to drain on a wire rack with a sheet of kitchen paper underneath to catch the drips.

When quite cool, roll the candied citron pieces in icing sugar and drop them into little paper cases.

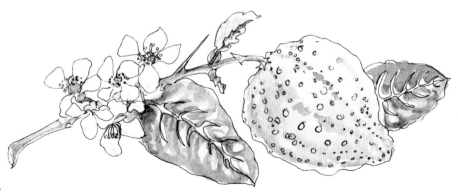

Jaén

ENDLESS OLIVE GROVES produce the culinary wealth of Jaén. The province serves as the geographical doorstep between Spain's high central plateau, the *meseta,* and the slopes of Andalucía. It was down the canyons of Despeñaperos in the north of Jaén that the Catholic Kings, Ferdinand of Aragon and Isabel of Castile, rode to reclaim Andalucía from the Moors.

Jaén is a golden city built of stone the colour of rich cream – not whitewashed like the rest of Andalucía. The poet Manuel Machado named it 'silvery Jaén', perhaps because of the pearl-pale trunks of its olive trees. To the north of the city, the Sierra de Jabalucz rises towards Castile, betraying in its name the *taifa,* the Moorish administrative area, which held the city. To the east, the beautiful forest-clad Sierra de Cazorla is now a wildlife sanctuary. The twin towns of Ubeda and Baeza are among the most graceful of Andalucía's citadels.

The cookery of this most mountain-bound of the provinces of Andalucía draws heavily on the potato, both as an accompaniment for meat and fish, and as a dish in its own right in combination with small quantities of more expensive ingredients, rather as rice or pasta is used in those areas which produce these other ingredients. The New World tuber, once the secret weapon of the Incas, has always flourished where lesser staples take a rain-check.

Jaén's most original dishes are those made with vegetables, although these are not necessarily the ones most frequently encountered in public eateries. The cookery of the province reflects in large measure that of her neighbours. La Mancha holds sway in the north and east with slow-cooked *cocidos* (soup-stews) and an excellent local version of Spain's own ratatouille, the *pisto manchego*. The south likes the spicings and herbs of Granada – with a bit of mint to underline the Moorish connection. In the west, the housewife looks towards the traditions of Córdoba.

Jaén's olive groves often have a catch crop of vegetables grown between the lines of silvery trees. Without the availability of fresh fish for the oil to fry, the rich juice of the olive is used in this region as an enrichment and seasoning in stews, vegetable dishes and salad – and also in celebration breads and cakes, in which it takes the place of the northern European butter.

The main business of Jaén's province has long been the exploitation of her minerals. Nevertheless, the land left for cultivation produces excellent fruit: Alcaudete is famous for its peaches, Jimena de Jaén has grenadines, Ubeda has plums, Quesada has figs, and Jandulillo is famous for its pears. Fruit naturally concludes the meal, as it does all over Andalucía, with the usual sweet biscuits and cakes saved for high days and holidays.

Sopa de cuarto de hora
Fifteen-minute broth

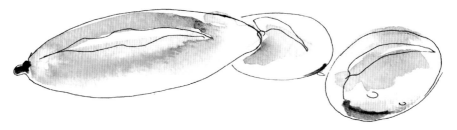

2 pints/1.2 litres/5 cups chicken, meat or vegetable stock (home-made is best, but a good stock cube will do)

1 large potato, cut into cubes the size of chickpeas, or a handful of soup noodles (the very thin ones)

4oz/125g *jamón serrano* cured ham, Parma ham or lean bacon

2 hard-boiled eggs, peeled and chopped

To finish

2 tablespoons chopped parsley

1-2 spring onions (scallions), finely chopped

Serves 4 as a starter

There are many variations of this light, fresh soup which can be quickly prepared with the stock from an old boiling fowl (the stock from Puchero con verduras *on page 161 is excellent). Some like to slide the egg raw into each portion of boiling soup when it is in the plate, so that the egg white just sets in the hot liquid.*

Bring the stock to the boil. Stir in the potato cubes or noodles and the ham or bacon. Bring back to the boil, and cook for long enough to soften the potato or noodles, whichever you are using.

Stir in the chopped eggs and bring back to the boil again. Ladle into soup plates. Finish with a sprinkling of parsley and spring onions (scallions).

Espinacas al estilo de Jaén
Spinach with breadcrumbs

1lb/500g fresh spinach,
** (or use frozen)**
6 tablespoons olive oil
2 garlic cloves, skinned
** and roughly chopped**
1 thick slice of bread,
** cut into cubes**
4 dried red peppers,
** de-seeded and soaked**
** for 2 hours, or 1 fresh**
** red pepper, hulled and**
** de-seeded**
2 tablespoons *pimentón*
Salt and pepper

Serves 4 as a starter,
* 2 as a main course*

This is probably Jaén's most distinctive dish. It is served on its own, either as a first course, or as a vegetarian main meal, maybe with a fried egg or two.

Rinse, pick over, shred and cook the fresh spinach leaves in a lidded pan with a little salt and the minimum of water for about 5 minutes. Frozen spinach must be defrosted first.

Meanwhile, heat the oil in a small frying-pan (skillet). Add the garlic and fry it until it softens and takes a little colour, then transfer it to a food processor or pestle and mortar.

Fry the bread cubes in the remaining oil until they are golden. Add them to the garlic, along with the flesh of the soaked dried red pepper scraped from its thin skin. If you are using a fresh pepper, chop and fry it until it softens, and then add it and the *pimentón* to the fried bread and garlic. Add a little water, process or pound to a paste and season.

Drain the spinach and turn it in the hot oil left in the pan, then stir in the paste. Turn down the heat, cover loosely, and simmer gently for 15-20 minutes to marry the flavours.

Serve, hot or cold, with fried or toasted bread rubbed with garlic.

THE FLAVOURS OF ANDALUCÍA

Puchero con verduras

Bean stew with greens

1lb/500g white haricot
 beans, soaked for a few
 hours or overnight
½ chicken, jointed
 (an old boiling fowl has
 the best flavour, but a
 young one will do)
½ garlic head (about
 6 cloves, in a lump)
2-3 thick-cut rashers
 salted pork belly,
 or unsmoked bacon,
 cubed
1 short length *jamón
 serrano* ham bone or
 piece of bacon knuckle
2 dried red peppers,
 de-seeded and torn, or 1
 fresh red pepper, hulled,
 de-seeded and sliced
1-2 large carrots, scraped
 and cut into chunks
1-2 turnips, peeled and
 cut into chunks
4 tablespoons olive oil
8-10 peppercorns,
 crushed
1-2 bay leaves
2 large potatoes, peeled
 and sliced
1lb/500g greens (spinach,
 chard, cabbage, kale or
 turnip tops), chopped
Salt and pepper

To finish (optional)
1-2 hard-boiled eggs,
 peeled and quartered

Serves 5-6

There is no defined recipe for a puchero, *the daily dish of Andalucía. It is an opportunist soup-stew, a veritable culinary magpie, based on a pulse vegetable combined with whatever ingredients the landscape, season and household budget dictate. Chickpeas claim the historical priority, but I prefer the alternative, haricot beans.*

Sometimes the dish can be nearly meatless, flavoured only with a chunk of ham bone, or a small piece of pork. If an elderly hen is used, any unlaid eggs found in her body cavity go into the dish at the end: they look rather alarming on the poultry stall in the market, winking in their tray like so many yellow eyes. Country housewives are far too close to their raw materials to let anything go to waste.

Drain the beans, put them in a heavy saucepan and pour in enough cold water to submerge them to a depth of two fingers. If the chicken is for boiling, it can go in now, otherwise save it for later. Do not skin the garlic or separate the cloves, but hold the whole head in a flame to char the paper covering and roast the cloves a little. Drop them into the saucepan along with the salt pork or bacon cubes, the ham or bacon bone, the dried red pepper pieces or fresh red pepper slices, the carrot and turnip chunks, olive oil, crushed peppercorns and bay leaves. Bring to the boil, and then turn down to a fast simmer. Cover loosely and cook for 1½-3 hours, adding extra boiling water, if necessary.

When the beans are soft but still firm, add the joints of chicken, unless you are using a boiling fowl. Bring back to the boil. After 20 minutes add the potatoes. When the potatoes are nearly soft, stir in the greens, turn up the heat, and simmer for another 5 minutes. To finish, taste and add salt, if necessary (the salt pork will have made it quite salty), and pepper, and stir in an extra spoonful of olive oil.

Serve the broth first and the meat and vegetables as a second course, topped with hard-boiled egg quarters, Andaluz-style.

Ajilimójili

Bits and pieces

1lb/500g potatoes
4 dried red peppers,
    soaked and torn,
    or 2 fresh red peppers,
    hulled, de-seeded and
    sliced
Salt
¼ pint/150ml/⅔ cup
    olive oil
1 tablespoon chopped
    mint
Cayenne

Serves 4 as a starter

This is one of the most popular of Jaén's vegetable dishes – certainly it is one frequently encountered on restaurant menus, including that of Jaén's handsome re-built Parador. The name of the dish means odds and ends, buttons and bows. Serve it as a starter – it is a kind of pâté made with red peppers, potato and oil pounded together.

Peel and slice the potatoes. Put them in a saucepan with the dried or fresh peppers. Cover with cold water, add salt and bring everything to the boil. Turn down the heat, cover and cook for 15-20 minutes, until the potatoes are tender.

Drain the potatoes and peppers, and mash everything to a fine puree, using a food processor, pestle and mortar, or a sieve and the back of a spoon. Beat in the olive oil, and season with salt and cayenne.

Pile up the puree on a pretty dish, finish with a sprinkle of chopped mint, and serve it at room temperature, with crisp lettuce leaves and hunks of bread for dipping. Alternatively, spread it on toast and serve as a tapa with a glass of red wine.

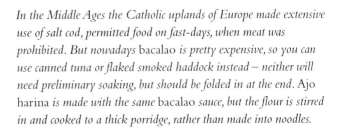

Andrajos
Noodles with salt cod

For the salt cod
8oz/250g salt cod
   (bacalao), soaked for
   24–48 hours with the
   water changed twice
4 tablespoons olive oil
1 onion, skinned and
   chopped
2 garlic cloves, skinned
1lb/500g tomatoes,
   scalded and skinned
   (or use canned)
2 dried red peppers, de-
   seeded and soaked, or
   3 tablespoons *pimentón*
2lb/1kg clams in the shell,
   soaked overnight in
   clean water (optional)
1 mint sprig, chopped
6 peppercorns
4-5 saffron threads
   (or ½ teaspoon ground
   saffron)

For the noodles
12oz/350g/3 cups strong
   bread flour
1 tablespoon salt
1 tablespoon olive oil
⅓ pint/250ml/1 cup
   water

Serves 4–5

In the Middle Ages the Catholic uplands of Europe made extensive use of salt cod, permitted food on fast-days, when meat was prohibited. But nowadays bacalao *is pretty expensive, so you can use canned tuna or flaked smoked haddock instead – neither will need preliminary soaking, but should be folded in at the end. Ajo harina is made with the same* bacalao *sauce, but the flour is stirred in and cooked to a thick porridge, rather than made into noodles.*

Drain the salt cod *(bacalao)* and pat it dry. Remove the skin and any bones.

Make the noodle dough. Sieve the flour into a large bowl with the salt. Work in the oil and enough water to make a soft dough. Work the dough well, then leave it to rest under a cloth for 20 minutes. On a well-floured board, roll the dough out very thinly, and cut it into smallish squares. Sprinkle with flour, cover with a cloth, and leave to rest for a little longer.

Meanwhile, warm the oil in a flameproof earthenware casserole or heavy frying-pan (skillet) and add the onion and one of the garlic cloves. Let it fry for 5-6 minutes until it is soft and lightly caramelized. Add the tomato and the flesh of the red peppers scraped off the skin, or the *pimentón*. Let it all bubble up to thicken the sauce: the time this takes depends on the wateriness of the tomatoes.

When the sauce is well concentrated, stir in the flaked salt cod and the clams, if using. Bring to the boil, cover and cook for 4-5 minutes until the shellfish open in the steam.

Pound the remaining garlic clove with the peppercorns and saffron in a mortar, dilute the paste with a splash of hot water, and stir it into the sauce and fish. Dilute the sauce with 2 cups of boiling water. Bubble it all up again, and slip in the noodle squares. Simmer for 4-5 minutes, until the noodles are soft. Taste for seasoning.

Serve in deep soup plates, with a spoon and fork, and bread for mopping juices and wiping fingers.

Bacalao con patatas bravas
Salt cod with potatoes and peppers

1lb/500g salt cod
  (bacalao), soaked for
  24-48 hours with the
  water changed twice
8 tablespoons olive oil
2 garlic cloves, chopped
2 red peppers, hulled,
  de-seeded and cut into
  strips
1lb/500g tomatoes,
  scalded, skinned and
  chopped
1 bay leaf
½ teaspoon ground
  cloves
½ teaspoon cumin seeds
½ teaspoon white pepper
1lb/500g potatoes, peeled
  and cubed
Salt and pepper

To finish
1 teaspoon *pimentón*
  (and a little cayenne if
  you like it hot)
1 tablespoon chopped
  parsley

Serves 4

If you cannot easily find salt cod, or the cost is too high – bacalao has long since ceased to be poor man's meat – any salt fish will do, including smoked haddock and salmon. Neither will need overnight soaking, of course, and the taste will not be quite the same; but the final dish will be fine.

Drain the salt cod and pat it dry. Remove the skin and any bones. Put the fish in a saucepan with enough cold water to cover it. Bring it to the boil and then set aside.

Warm the oil in a heavy frying-pan (skillet). Add the chopped garlic and peppers and let them fry gently until they soften and take a little colour. Stir in the tomatoes with the bay leaf, cloves, cumin and white pepper and let it all bubble up. Add the potato cubes and enough hot water to submerge everything. Bring to the boil, turn down the heat, cover loosely and let it simmer gently until the potatoes are soft and most of the liquid has evaporated – 15-20 minutes should do the trick. Drain off any excess liquid.

Mash the potatoes well with the tomatoes and pepper – taste and add salt, if necessary, and pepper, but don't forget that the fish itself is pretty salty.

Drain the salt cod – you can add some of the cooking water to the mashed potato if the mixture looks too thick – and arrange the fish on top of the potato in the frying-pan.

Reheat, finish with a sprinkle of *pimentón* and chopped parsley, and serve.

Some people like the serving order reversed: the salt cod with the peppered potato on top like a sauce – in which case the mash should be more runny.

Pipirrana

Vegetable dip

1lb/500g green peppers,
    hulled and de-seeded
8oz/250g tomatoes
½ cucumber
Spanish onion, skinned
6 tablespoons olive oil
2 tablespoons vinegar
1 teaspoon cumin seeds
Salt and pepper

Serves 4 as a starter

This is a chopped salad which makes a delicious dip as a first course. You can include hard-boiled eggs, canned tuna or pickled fish if you like. There are no rules: mother knows best, so make up your own. If you can find those thin-fleshed green peppers grown specially for frying, make the dish with those, either raw or fried.

Chop all the raw vegetables finely. Mix them with the oil and vinegar. Roast the cumin briefly in a dry pan, then add it to the vegetables. Season with salt and pepper and leave the mixture to infuse for a few hours.

Serve with bread and cos lettuce leaves, as a dip. It also makes a fine topping for a baked potato in the winter, and a good dressing for a dish of new potatoes in the summer.

Alboronia

Vegetable casserole

1lb/500g aubergines (eggplants), hulled and diced

Salt and pepper

6 tablespoons olive oil

1 large Spanish onion, skinned and chopped

2 garlic cloves, skinned and chopped

8oz/250g green peppers, hulled, de-seeded and cut into strips

8oz/250g pumpkin or marrow

1–2 bay leaves

8oz/250g ripe tomatoes, scalded, skinned and chopped

1 tablespoon fresh breadcrumbs

Serves 4

The local version of this basic vegetable stew, the pisto manchego of Jaén's neighbours, adds yellow marrow, onion and aubergine (eggplant) to the favourite dish of La Mancha. Compare it to the Provençal ratatouille: the Mediterranean is a small world.

Put the diced aubergine (eggplant) in a colander and lightly salt it. Leave it for 20 minutes or so to draw out the vegetable's bitter juices.

Heat the olive oil in a deep frying-pan (skillet). Add the diced aubergine and the chopped onion and garlic and let them fry gently until they take a little colour. Push all to one side and add the sliced peppers and let them fry gently. Push to one side. Dice the pumpkin or marrow and add it to the pan with the bay leaves. Season with salt and plenty of freshly milled black pepper. Let everything fry gently (you may need to add another tablespoon of oil), until the vegetables are soft.

Stir in the chopped tomatoes, turn up the heat and let the sauce bubble fiercely for a few minutes to evaporate off any excess moisture and thicken the sauce.

Stir in the breadcrumbs to finish the thickening. Serve as a starter, or on its own as a light supper dish, topping each portion with an egg, either fried or hard-boiled and peeled and quartered.

Rollo de romería
Pilgrimage pâté

2lb/1kg minced pork
   and beef
4oz/125g *jamón serrano*
   cured ham or lean
   gammon, finely
   chopped
2 eggs, lightly forked
3oz/75g/1 cup fresh
   breadcrumbs
1 teaspoon ground cumin
Salt and pepper
1 tablespoon plain
   (all-purpose) flour
2 hard-boiled eggs,
   peeled
2 tablespoons oil
2-3 slices bacon, roughly
   chopped, rind and all
1 bay leaf
1 glass dry sherry
   or white wine

Serves 5-6

This is picnic food – traditional to the romería *to the shrine of the Virgin Patroness of Baños de la Encina. All round the Mediterranean, the Holy Mother of God has inherited from the old pagan goddesses the care of the springs which feed the wells of the villages and towns. So these annual summer pilgrimages to fetch the Lady of the Mountains to spend time with her congregation in the valley have an ancient and very practical purpose. The meat roll is quite difficult to handle – if preferred, chill it overnight before cooking it.*

Mix the minced pork and beef, the ham or gammon, the eggs, breadcrumbs, cumin, a little salt and plenty of pepper, and work into a firm paste.

Lightly flour a clean cloth and lay on half the meat mixture in a long flat sausage. Lay the hard-boiled eggs down the middle and cover with the remaining meat mixture. Dust with a little more flour and roll it up with the help of the cloth to make a fat roll.

Warm the oil in a saucepan just large enough to accommodate the meat roll. When it is hot, put in the roll and turn it carefully so that it browns a little on all sides.

Add the bacon, bay leaf, sherry or wine, and enough water to nearly cover the roll. Bring to the boil, turn down the heat, cover and leave to simmer gently for an hour or so. Test with a skewer: when the juices run clear, it is ready.

To take on the *romería* or on a picnic, let the roll cool overnight in its own juices. Slice it and wrap it up in a cloth. If you would like it hot, serve it cut in slices overlapped in a circle, with fresh tomato sauce poured in the middle.

Picadillo con jamón
Saffron mincemeat with ham

1½lb/750g minced meat
   (best done by hand
   with a knife, if you
   have time)
4oz/125g unsmoked
   streaky bacon, finely
   chopped
2oz/50g *jamón serrano*
   cured ham or Parma
   ham, finely chopped
2 tablespoons olive oil
6 peppercorns
1 garlic clove, skinned
5-6 saffron threads
   (or ½ teaspoon ground
   saffron)
1 tablespoon chopped
   parsley
1lb/500g potatoes,
   peeled and cubed
1 bay leaf
Salt and pepper

To finish
4 hard-boiled eggs,
   peeled and sliced

Serves 4

This is Monday mince with Moorish spicing – it certainly beats school mince. Spanish meat is well flavoured but inclined to be tough, which makes it the perfect candidate for mincing. Spanish butchers will do this for you on demand, allowing the housewife to select, say, a bit of fat pork and a piece of beef skirt, and have them put through the mincer to produce exactly the mixture she likes for her family's favourite recipe. Vary the proportions of minced meat, bacon and ham as you please.

Mix the minced meat with the bacon and ham. Warm the oil in a flameproof earthenware casserole or heavy saucepan. When hot, stir in the meats and brown them a little.

Meanwhile, crush the peppercorns with the garlic, saffron and parsley, dilute with a splash of water and stir this paste into the minced meat as it fries.

Stir in the potato cubes and turn them with the meat. Tuck in the bay leaf, and pour in enough water to submerge everything. Bring to the boil, turn down the heat, cover loosely and leave to simmer gently for 25-30 minutes, until the meat is tender and the potatoes are soft.

Taste and season with salt and pepper, let it bubble up to evaporate off any excess moisture, then pile it all up on a pretty dish – unless you have cooked it in a casserole, in which case serve it in the dish in which it was cooked. Finish with slices of hard-boiled egg.

THE FLAVOURS OF ANDALUCÍA

Biscocho

Madeira cake with olive oil and anis

4 eggs

8oz/250g/2 cups plain (all-purpose) flour

2 teaspoons baking powder

½ teaspoon salt

1 teaspoon ground cinnamon

8 floz/250ml/1 cup olive oil

8oz/200g/1 cup caster (superfine) sugar

1 tablespoon anis seeds

Serves 6

This cake is very easy to make. All the main ingredients – oil, flour, sugar – should weigh the same as the eggs, and large eggs weigh about 2oz/50g each. It's popular all over Spain although the inclusion of the anis seeds makes it particularly gienense.

Whisk the eggs lightly together in a small bowl. Sieve the flour, baking powder, salt and cinnamon into a large bowl. With a wooden spoon, beat in the eggs and all the other ingredients, until the mixture is smooth and free of lumps.

Oil a loaf tin (pan) measuring 9¼ x 5¼ x 3 inches/23 x 12.5 x 7.5 cm and line the base with greaseproof paper. Tip in the mixture and spread it into the corners.

Bake the cake in the oven at 350°F, 180°C, Gas Mark 4 for 1½ hours, until it is well risen, firm when pressed with the finger and has shrunk from the sides of the tin. Transfer it to a wire rack to cool.

Biscochos hornazos de pascua
Easter egg buns

1lb/500g strong white bread (all-purpose) flour
1 teaspoon salt
1oz/25g fresh yeast (or ½oz/15g dried yeast, following the instructions on the packet)
1 teaspoon sugar
About ½ pint/300ml/ 1¼ cups warm water
4 tablespoons olive oil
1 tablespoon anis seeds

To finish
8 red-dyed hard-boiled eggs (add *cochineal* to the cooking water)
1 egg, lightly forked
2-3 tablespoons sugar

Makes 8 buns

Eggs were forbidden in Lent – a limitation which had little meaning in the barnyard. If all the eggs laid by broody hens were allowed to hatch, there would be too many chicks. The solution was to hard-boil the extra eggs and store them up for eating later, at Easter. Egg pastries and bread with dyed hard-boiled eggs set round the rim are to be found in various forms all over Catholic Europe. As a prudent housewife myself, I suspect that dyeing the eggs was originally a way to distinguish the cooked from the raw, rather than a religious gesture.

Sieve the flour with the salt into a warm bowl. Blend the fresh yeast with the sugar in a blender or food processor, and mix it with half the water. Pour this liquid into a hollow in the flour and put it in a warm place for 10 minutes for the yeast to start working. When the yeast is bubbling, pour in most of the remaining water (you may not need it all, or you may need a little more) and work in the flour with your hand until you have a smooth soft dough. (If using dried yeast, get to this stage following the directions on the packet.) Knead the dough thoroughly on a well-floured board. Return the dough ball to the bowl, cover it with a damp cloth, and put it to rise in a warm place for 1-2 hours.

Heat the oil in a small frying-pan (skillet). Take it off the heat when it starts bubbling and stir in the anis seeds. Let it cool to blood temperature. When the dough has doubled its bulk, knock it down, kneading well. Flour the board again and work the warm oil and anis seeds into the dough, using extra flour as you need it.

Divide two-thirds of the dough into eight pieces. Roll these out into *tortas* (rounds) about 3-4 inches/7.5-10 cm wide and ¾ inch/2 cm thick and transfer them to a well-oiled baking sheet. Make dents in the middle of each round and insert a red egg. Place strips of the remaining dough in a cross over each egg, and stick the ends down with a little water. Put the buns to rise again for about 20 minutes, then brush with egg and sprinkle with sugar. Bake in the oven at 400°F, 200°C, Gas Mark 6 for 25-30 minutes, until well risen and golden brown. Serve them with hot milky coffee spiked with a splash of anis brandy.

Tortas al hoyo
Honey and sesame biscuits

1lb/500g/4 cups plain
   (all-purpose) flour
½ teaspoon salt
8oz/250g lard
   or margarine
8oz/250g/1 cup sugar
2 eggs, lightly forked
Juice of 1 lemon
1 jar thick honey
2oz/50g sesame seeds

Makes about 30 biscuits

These belong to the large family of polvorones, mantecados and other rich powdery biscuits which are a speciality of Christmas. Good children hope to find a handful of them tucked into their shoes on 6 January, the day the Three Kings brought their gifts to the Christ Child, and on which they now bring presents to lesser mortals.

Sieve the flour and salt into a bowl. In a separate bowl, beat the lard or margarine with the sugar, eggs and lemon juice. Work in enough flour to give a smooth, soft dough. Let it rest in a cool place for 15 minutes, covered with a cloth.

Flour a board thoroughly, and roll out the dough to ¾ inch/ 1 cm thick. Using a floured wineglass, cut out circles of dough, and transfer them to a greased baking tray.

Make a hollow in each biscuit with a well-floured thumb, and use a spoon to drop a little honey into each dent. Sprinkle with sesame seeds.

Bake in the oven at 350°F, 180°C, Gas Mark 4 for about 20 minutes, until golden. Transfer the biscuits to a wire rack to cool; they are soft when hot and crisp when cool. Store, wrapped in scraps of tissue paper, in an airtight tin.

Index

THE FLAVOURS OF ANDALUCÍA